Titus

Preaching Verse-by-Verse

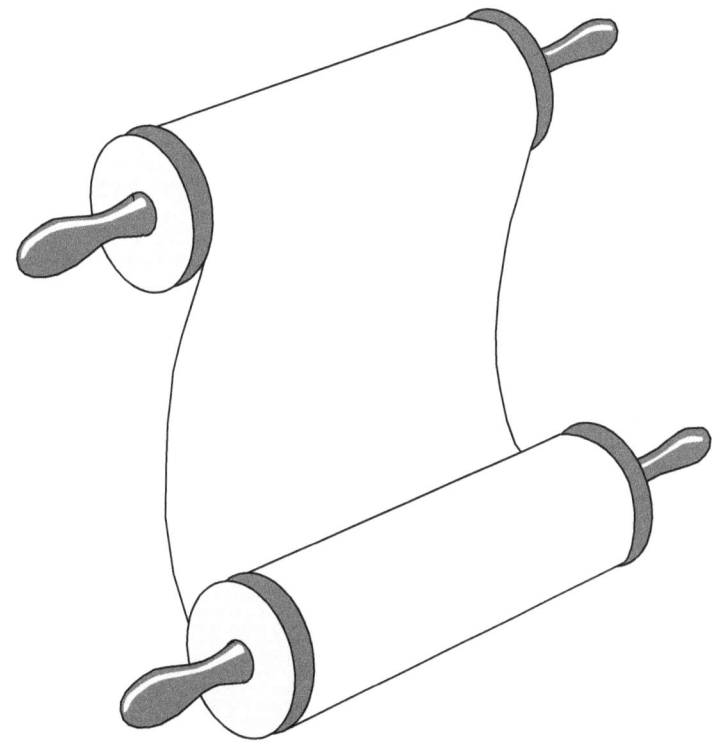

Pastor D. A. Waite, Th.D., Ph.D.

Published by
THE BIBLE FOR TODAY PRESS

Published by
THE BIBLE FOR TODAY PRESS
900 Park Avenue
Collingswood, New Jersey 08108 U.S.A.
Pastor D. A. Waite, Th.D., Ph.D.
Bible For Today Baptist Church
Church Phone: 856-854-4747
BFT Phone: 856-854-4452
Orders: 1-800-John 10:9
e-mail: BFT@BibleForToday.org
Website: www.BibleForToday.org
FAX: 856-854-2464

We Use and Defend
the King James Bible

Copyright, 2017
All Rights Reserved
August, 2017

BFT #4166

ISBN #978-1-56848-114-2

Acknowledgments

I wish to thank and to acknowledge the assistance of the following people:

- **The Congregation of the Bible For Today Baptist Church**–for whom these messages were prepared, to whom they were delivered, and by whom they were published. They listened attentively and encouraged their Pastor.
- **Yvonne Sanborn Waite**–my wife, who encouraged the publication of these sermons, read the manuscript, developed the various boxes, and gave other helpful suggestions and comments. The boxes help the reader to see some of the more important topics that are covered in the various chapters.
- **Pastor Daniel Waite**–our church's Assistant Pastor for helping to keep our computers up-to-date and working properly day by day so that this book could be written and published.
- **Patricia Canter**–a friend of Mrs. Waite and me who volunteered to take the cassette tapes of the verse-by-verse exposition of the book of James and put these words into the computer in digital format to be used for this book. She also volunteered help with the final step of proofreading the entire book once the first draft was completed. Without her assistance, this books and many other books she has worked on could not be completed for publication.
- **Dr. Kirk DiVietro**–a friend for many years, one of our Dean Burgon Society faithful Vice Presidents, who is an expert on the use of computers. He has helped in various ways to make the computer work easier and in the proper manner when performing the tasks needed to complete this book.

Foreword

- **The Beginning.** This book is the **fifteenth** in a series of verse-by-verse preaching from various New Testament books of the Bible. It is an attempt to bring to the minds of the readers two things: (1) the **meaning** of the words in the verses, and (2) some practical **applications** of those words to the lives of both genuine Christians and non-Christians.
- **Preached Sermons.** These were messages that I preached to our **Bible For Today Baptist Church** in Collingswood, New Jersey. They were broadcast over the Internet by computer streaming around the world. I took half a chapter each Sunday as the messages were preached. All verses quoted are from the King James Bible.
- **Other Verses.** In connection with both the **meaning** and **application** of the verses in this book, there are many verses from other places in the Bible that have been quoted for further elaboration on the teachings in this book. All the verses of Scripture that were used to illustrate further truth are written out in full for easy reference.
- **A Transcription.** This entire book was typed into computer format by Patricia Canter from the tape recordings of the messages as they were preached. In addition to the words used as I preached these sermons, I have added other words for clarification as needed.
- **The Audience.** The intended audience for this book is the same as the audience that listened to the messages in the first place. These studies are not meant to be overly scholarly, though there are some references to various Greek or Hebrew Words used. My aim and burden is to try to help genuine Christians to understand and follow the Words of God. It is also my hope that my children, grandchildren, great grandchildren, and others might profit from this study. There is an **11-page INDEX** of words and phrases to help the reader easily find the various topics they are looking for.

Yours For God's Words,

D. A. Waite

Pastor D. A. Waite, Th.D., Ph.D.
Bible For Today Baptist Church

Table of Contents

Publisher's Data. I
Acknowledgments. ii
Foreword.. iii
Table of Contents. iv
Titus Chapter One. 1
Titus Chapter Two. 41
Titus Chapter Three.. 81
Index of Words and Phrases.. 113
About the Author. 125
Order Blank Pages. 127
Defined King James Bible Orders. 135

Titus
Chapter One

Titus 1:1

"Paul, a servant of God, and an apostle of Jesus Christ, according to the faith of God's elect, and the acknowledging of the truth which is after godliness;"

Titus was a pastor in the small island of Crete. The Apostle Paul was writing to him with instructions on how best to pastor his church. Paul identifies himself as both a *"servant of God"* and also an *"apostle of Jesus Christ."*

THE MEANING OF THE GREEK WORD, DOULOS

The Greek Word for *"servant"* is DOULOS. Some of the meanings of this Greek Word are:

> *"1) a slave, bondman, man of servile condition; 1a) a slave; 1b) metaph., one who gives himself up to another's will those whose service is used by Christ in extending and advancing His cause among men; 1c) devoted to another to the disregard of one's own interests; 2) a servant, attendant; It speaks of servants who give themselves up to do another's will."*

CHRISTIANS SHOULD BE DEVOTED TO CHRIST

Genuine Christians should be devoted to the Lord Jesus Christ with a disregard for their own interests.

Three men are called *"servants of God"* in the King James Bible:
1. Paul (Titus 1:1)
2. James (James 1:1)
3. Moses (Revelation 15:3

Paul was also an apostle. The word, "*apostle,*" is used 19 times in the New Testament of our King James Bible. Sixteen of those times, it's used of the Apostle Paul.

Titus 1:2

"In hope of eternal life, which God, that cannot lie, promised before the world began;"

THE OFFER OF ETERNAL LIFE

Paul is speaking in this verse about eternal life which is offered to everyone who genuinely believes that the Lord Jesus Christ died for their sins (John 3:16 and many other verses). This eternal life is a hope that is future, yet certain. It has been promised by the God of the Bible Who "*cannot lie.*"

Verses On Hope

- **Romans 15:4**

"For whatsoever things were written aforetime were written for our learning, that we through patience and comfort of the scriptures might have hope."

Both the Old and the New Testament Scriptures give genuine Christians hope.

- **Romans 15:13**

"Now the God of hope fill you with all joy and peace in believing, that ye may abound in hope, through the power of the Holy Ghost."

One of the titles for the God of the Bible is "*the God of hope.*"

- **Colossians 1:5**

"For the hope which is laid up for you in heaven, whereof ye heard before in the word of the truth of the gospel;"

NON-CHRISTIANS DESTINED TO HELL

True born-again Christians have a hope in heaven. There is no such hope for the non-Christian multitudes. They are destined to the Lake of Fire in Hell.

- **Titus 2:13**

"Looking for that blessed hope, and the glorious appearing of the great God and our Saviour Jesus Christ;"

The first part of this verse, "*that blessed hope*" refers to coming of the Lord Jesus Christ in the air, to snatch away all genuine Christians in the rapture.

Verses On God's Promises

- **Numbers 23:19**

"God *is* not a man, that he should lie; neither the son of man, that he should repent: hath he said, and shall he not do *it*? or hath he spoken, and shall he not make it good?"

Throughout the course of history people have made promises they have no intention of keeping. President Obama was such a man who lied about many, many important matters. God is not like that. He always keeps His promises.

- **Romans 4:20-21**

"He [Abraham] staggered not at the promise of God through unbelief; but was strong in faith, giving glory to God; And being fully persuaded that, what he had promised, he was able also to perform."

Abraham fully trusted in God's promises and acted upon them. God not only promises, but fulfills His promises in every detail.

- **Hebrews 10:23**

"Let us hold fast the profession of *our* faith without wavering; (for he *is* faithful that promised;)"

God is faithful in keeping all of His promises.

- **1 John 2:25**

"And this is the promise that he hath promised us, *even* eternal life."

GENUINE TRUST IN CHRIST GIVES ETERNAL LIFE

If people genuinely trust in the Lord Jesus Christ as their Saviour, God will keep His promise in giving them eternal life.

- **John 3:16**

"For God so loved the world, that he gave his only begotten Son, that whosoever believeth in him should not perish, but have everlasting life."

God will keep that promise as well. He's not like many human beings who fail to keep their promises.

Titus 1:3

"But hath in due times manifested his word through preaching, which is committed unto me according to the commandment of God our Saviour;"

PREACHERS SHOULD PREACH BIBLE DOCTRINES

God has manifested His Word through preaching. It is imperative that preachers should preach the Words of God to their congregations. It is very unfortunate that preachers in this country and all around the world are preaching doctrines that are contrary to that which is taught in the Words of God.

Verses On Preaching

- **Matthew 4:17**

"From that time Jesus began to preach, and to say, Repent: for the kingdom of heaven is at hand."

Even the Lord Jesus Christ preached on various topics when He was on the earth.

- **Matthew 10:27**

"What I tell you in darkness, *that* speak ye in light: and what ye hear in the ear, *that* preach ye upon the housetops."

The disciples of the Lord Jesus Christ were told to preach to all people the message that He told them.

- **Matthew 12:41**

"The men of Nineveh shall rise in judgment with this generation, and shall condemn it: because they repented at the preaching of Jonas; and, behold, a greater than Jonas *is* here."

When Jonah preached to Nineveh that they were going to be judged by the Lord, they repented of their wickedness.

- **Mark 16:15**

"And he said unto them, Go ye into all the world, and preach the gospel to every creature."

The Gnostic Critical Greek Text removed Mark 16:9-20, including this verse 15. Because of this, the command of the Lord Jesus Christ to *"preach the gospel to every creature"* is omitted by such versions as the American Standard Version, New American Standard Version, New International Version, Revised Standard Version, the English

Standard Version, and by many, many other Bible versions, not only in English, but also in many other languages of the world.

- **Luke 24:47**
  "And that <u>repentance and remission of sins should be preached in his name among all nations</u>, beginning at Jerusalem."

THE APOSTLES PREACHED THE GOSPEL TO MANY

The apostles obeyed the commands of their Saviour and faithfully preached His gospel to many people.

- **Acts 5:42**
  "And daily in the temple, and in every house, <u>they ceased not to teach and preach Jesus Christ</u>."

Though these apostles were persecuted by the rulers of their day, they continued to teach and preach the gospel of the Lord Jesus Christ.

Acts 8:4
"Therefore they that were scattered abroad went every where <u>preaching the word</u>."

PERSECUTION SCATTERED THE CHRISTIANS

Because of their persecution, the apostles were scattered everywhere and continued preaching God's Words.

- **Acts 8:25**
  "And they, when they had testified and <u>preached the word of the Lord</u>, returned to Jerusalem, and <u>preached the gospel in many villages of the Samaritans</u>."

The apostles continued preaching the gospel in Jerusalem and in many villages of the Samaritans as well.

- **Acts 9:20**
  "And straightway <u>he preached Christ in the synagogues, that he is the Son of God</u>."

As soon as Paul was saved, immediately, he preached the gospel of the Lord Jesus Christ as the Son of God.

- **Romans 1:15**
  "So, as much as in me is, <u>I am ready to preach the gospel</u> to you that are at Rome also."

Paul was ready to preach the gospel to those in Rome as well as in other places.

- **Romans 10:14-15**

"How then shall they call on him in whom they have not believed? and how shall they believe in him of whom they have not heard? and how shall they hear without a preacher? And how shall they preach, except they be sent? as it is written, How beautiful are the feet of them that preach the gospel of peace, and bring glad tidings of good things!"

PREACHERS SHOULD BE CALLED BY GOD

Preachers should be called by God Himself as He directs them to preach the gospel of peace. Sad to say, many preachers are not sent by the Lord. It is also sad that many, many preachers are lost and bound for Hell. Their preaching is dangerous and can lead no one to accept the Lord Jesus Christ as their Saviour.

- **1 Corinthians 1:18**

"For the preaching of the cross is to them that perish foolishness; but unto us which are saved it is the power of God."

PREACHING ABOUT THE CROSS IS NEEDED

It is the preaching of what was accomplished at the cross of the Lord Jesus Christ that should be proclaimed by every godly preacher. It is that kind of preaching that is undergirded by the power of God.

- **1 Corinthians 1:21**

"For after that in the wisdom of God the world by wisdom knew not God, it pleased God by the foolishness of preaching to save them that believe."

Preaching, even though considered "*foolishness*" by some is the method God has given to save those who believe on the Lord Jesus Christ as their Saviour.

- **1 Corinthians 2:4-5**

"And my speech and my preaching *was* not with enticing words of man's wisdom, but in demonstration of the Spirit and of power: That your faith should not stand in the wisdom of men, but in the power of God."

Paul's preaching was a demonstration of God the Holy Spirit and His power. It was not with enticing words of man's wisdom.

- **1 Corinthians 9:16**
"For though I preach the gospel, I have nothing to glory of: for necessity is laid upon me; yea, woe is unto me, if I preach not the gospel!

Paul does not glory when he preaches the gospel. If he failed to preach the gospel woe would be on him.

- **1 Corinthians 15:1**
"Moreover, brethren, I declare unto you the gospel which I preached unto you, which also ye have received, and wherein ye stand;"

Paul declared the gospel he preached to those in the Corinthian church. They received that gospel and were standing upon it.

- **Ephesians 3:8**
"Unto me, who am less than the least of all saints, is this grace given, that I should preach among the Gentiles the unsearchable riches of Christ;"

The Lord Jesus Christ gave Paul His grace and enablement to preach to the Gentiles the unsearchable riches of Christ.

- **2 Timothy 4:2**
"Preach the word; be instant in season, out of season; reprove, rebuke, exhort with all longsuffering and doctrine."

MANY PREACHERS DO NOT PREACH GOD'S WORDS

Sound preachers preach God's Words, but there are multitudes of preachers who do not obey Paul's command to Pastor Timothy. Instead, they present talks either with no doctrinal content, or else with doctrines that contradict the Words of God.

- **1 Peter 1:25**
"But the word of the Lord endureth for ever. And this is the word which by the gospel is preached unto you."

Peter preached the true gospel of Christ. This gospel contains bad news as well as good news. The bad news is that all people are lost and bound for hell. The good news is the Lord Jesus Christ died for sinners and took the sins of the sinners upon Himself on the cross of Calvary. Those who truly trust Him, believe on Him, may receive everlasting life. That's the good news. Faithful, genuine faith in this gospel can save the soul from Hell and its eternal fires.

Titus 1:4

"To Titus, mine own son after the common faith: Grace, mercy, and peace, from God the Father and the Lord Jesus Christ our Saviour."

Paul now mentions Titus by name. He is called Paul's *"son after the common faith."* Evidently, Paul led Titus to genuine faith in the Lord Jesus Christ. Titus is now the pastor of the church on the island of Crete.

PAUL GREETS TITUS WITH GRACE, MERCY & PEACE

Paul greets Titus with three words: (1) grace, (2) mercy, and (3) peace. All three of these are gifts from God the Father and the Lord Jesus Christ. Notice that God the Father is here united with God the Son. Both are members of the Trinity. Apostate and ungodly ministers and lay people deny the Deity of the Lord Jesus Christ, believing that He is only a human being rather than God in the flesh.

Verses That Mention Titus

- **2 Corinthians 2:13**

"I had no rest in my spirit, because I found not Titus my brother: but taking my leave of them, I went from thence into Macedonia."

Paul wanted to find Titus, but didn't know where he was.

- **2 Corinthians 7:6**

"Nevertheless God, that comforteth those that are cast down, comforted us by the coming of Titus;"

Titus comforted Paul when he came to be with him. This was one of the gifts belonging to Pastor Titus.

- **2 Corinthians 7:13**

"Therefore we were comforted in your comfort: yea, and exceedingly the more joyed we for the joy of Titus, because his spirit was refreshed by you all."

Titus did not only comfort Paul, but Paul had exceeding joy because of the joy that Titus had.

- **2 Corinthians 8:6**

"Insomuch that we desired Titus, that as he had begun, so he would also finish in you the same grace also."

Paul is hoping that Titus would finish in the Corinthians the grace of giving to the Lord's work.
- **2 Corinthians 8:16**
"But thanks *be* to God, which put the same earnest care into the heart of Titus for you."

Paul mentioned that God gave Titus earnest care for the Corinthian Christians.
- **2 Corinthians 8:23**
"Whether any do enquire of Titus, he is my partner and fellowhelper concerning you: or our brethren be enquired of, they are the messengers of the churches, and the glory of Christ."

TITUS WAS PAUL'S HELPER
Titus was Paul's partner and fellowhelper in his ministry for the Lord Jesus Christ.

- **2 Corinthians 12:18**
"I desired Titus, and with *him* I sent a brother. Did Titus make a gain of you? walked we not in the same spirit? *walked we* not in the same steps?"

Titus didn't make any gain for himself from the Corinthian Christians. He didn't steal from them in any way.
- **Galatians 2:1**
"Then fourteen years after I went up again to Jerusalem with Barnabas, and took Titus with *me* also."

AFTER HIS SALVATION, PAUL WAS TAUGHT BY CHRIST
After Paul was saved by the Lord Jesus Christ, he went to the Arabian place and was taught by the Lord. Fourteen years later, he went to Jerusalem to meet with Peter and the other apostles. He took Titus with him on that occasion.

- **Galatians 2:3**
"But neither Titus, who was with me, being a Greek, was compelled to be circumcised:"

Titus, who was a Greek, was not compelled to be circumcised.

Titus 1:5

"**For this cause left I thee in Crete, that thou shouldest set in order the things that are wanting, and ordain elders in every city, as I had appointed thee:**"

Paul left Titus in Crete where he became the pastor of that church. Paul wanted him to do two things: (1) to set in order things that are lacking in that church, and (2) ordain pastors/bishops/elders in every city.

Even today, there are hundreds and even many thousands of churches (both in the USA and around the world) that need to be set in order according to the clear teachings of the Bible. These churches are out of order in many ways.

> **THE MEANING OF THE GREEK WORD, EPIDIORTHOO**
> The Greek Word for "*set in order*" is EPIDIORTHOO. Some of the meanings of that Greek Word are:
> "*put into order, straighten out, correct (Titus 1:5)*"

The second thing Paul wanted Titus to do was to "*ordain elders in every city.*" From a careful study of two clear passages of the New Testament, there is one man who is in charge of each local church. He has three titles. His three titles are: (1) Pastor, (2) Bishop, and (3) Elder.

The clear proof of this position of pastor/bishop/elder being the same person with different offices is found in a careful examination of the following two passages.

(1) Acts 22:17, 28   (Verse 17 below)

"*And from Miletus he sent to Ephesus, and* called the elders [**PRESBUTEROS**] *of the church*...." (Verse 28 below)

"... *Take heed therefore unto yourselves, and to all the flock, over the which the Holy Ghost hath made you* **overseers**, [bishops, **EPISKOPOS**] *to* **feed** [pastor, **POIMAINO**] *the church of God, which he hath purchased with his own blood.*"

(2) 1 Peter 5:1-2

"*The* **elders** [**PRESBUTEROS**] *which are among you I exhort, who am also an elder, and a witness of the sufferings of Christ, and also a partaker of the* *glory that shall be revealed:* **Feed** [pastor **POIMAINO**] *the flock of God which is among you, taking the **oversight** [bishop **EPISKOPOS**] thereof, not by constraint, but willingly; not for filthy lucre, but of a ready mind;"*

THE MEANING OF THE GREEK WORD, KATHISTEMI

The Greek Word for *"ordain"* is KATHISTEMI. Some of the meanings of that Greek Word are:

"appoint, put in charge, designate (Mt 24:45); cause to be, make (Ac 7:10, 27, 35; Ro 5:19)"

PASTORS ARE ORDAINED BY LOCAL CHURCHES

It is clear that Titus, as the pastor/bishop/elder of the local church or churches in Crete, was to ordain these men from the authority of that local church rather than from any higher-up group or organization such as a presbytery, a bishop, or some other entity. The local church was to be a sovereign and independent body.

Verses On "Set In Order"

- **Exodus 40:4**

"And thou shalt bring in the table, and set in order the things that are to be set in order upon it; and thou shalt bring in the candlestick, and light the lamps thereof."

All the various parts of the Old Testament tabernacle were to be set in their proper order as in the pattern which was given by the Lord.

- **Ecclesiastes 12:9**

"And moreover, because the preacher was wise, he still taught the people knowledge; yea, he gave good heed, and sought out, *and* set in order many proverbs."

Solomon was the author of thousands of proverbs which he set in order as God instructed and led him.

- **1 Corinthians 11:34**

"And if any man hunger, let him eat at home; that ye come not together unto condemnation. And the rest will I set in order when I come."

> **THE CORINTHIAN CHURCH WAS DISORDERLY**
> The Corinthian church was very disorderly at the Lord's supper. God judged many of them. Paul would set in order many of these wrong actions when he would visit them in the future.

Verses On Ordain

- **1 Chronicles 9:22**

"All these *which were* chosen to be porters in the gates *were* two hundred and twelve. These were reckoned by their genealogy in their villages, whom <u>David and Samuel the seer did ordain in their set office</u>."

David and Samuel ordained the porters for the temple in the proper order and place.

- **Jeremiah 1:5**

"Before I formed thee in the belly I knew thee; and before thou camest forth out of the womb I sanctified thee, *and* <u>I ordained thee a prophet unto the nations</u>."

The Lord ordained Jeremiah as a prophet.

- **Mark 3:14**

"And <u>he ordained twelve</u>, that they should be with him, and that he might send them forth to preach,"

The Lord Jesus Christ ordained the twelve apostles that they should be with Him and that they might be sent forth to preach.

- **John 15:16**

"Ye have not chosen me, but <u>I have</u> chosen you, and <u>ordained you, that ye should go and bring forth fruit</u>, and *that* your fruit should remain: that whatsoever ye shall ask of the Father in my name, he may give it you."

The Lord Jesus Christ ordained His apostles to go and bear fruit.

- **Acts 1:22**

"Beginning from the baptism of John, unto that same day that he was taken up from us, must <u>one be ordained to be a witness with us of his resurrection</u>."

> **PETER'S SELECTING MATTHIAS WAS IN ERROR**
>
> I believe Peter's personal decision to ordain someone to take the place of Judas Iscariot was in error. The Holy Spirit had not yet empowered the apostles. Because of this, they made a wrong choice. The Lord Jesus Christ chose Paul to be his apostle just as he had chosen the former twelve to be His apostles.

- Acts 14:23

"And <u>when they had ordained them elders in every church</u>, and had prayed with fasting, they commended them to the Lord, on whom they believed."

Pastors-bishops-elders were ordained in every church.

- 1 Timothy 2:7

"Whereunto <u>I am ordained a preacher, and an apostle</u>, (I speak the truth in Christ, *and* lie not;) a teacher of the Gentiles in faith and verity."

Paul was ordained by the Lord Jesus Christ to be both a preacher and an apostles.

Titus 1:6

"If any be blameless, the husband of one wife, having faithful children not accused of riot or unruly."

In these next verses, there are to be a total of fifteen Biblical qualifications before any local church should ordain their pastors to the gospel ministry.

    1. **The First Biblical Qualification For A Pastor Is That He Is Blameless.**

> **THE MEANING OF THE GREEK WORD, ANEGKLETOS**
>
> The Greek Word for *"blameless"* is ANEGKLETOS. Some of the meanings of this Greek Word are:
>
> ἀνέγκλητος   blameless, free from accusation (1Co 1:8; Col 1:22; 1Ti 3:10; Tit 1:6, 7)

Another important addition from another Greek Lexicon about *"free from accusation"* is that it must be an **untrue** accusation. That should be added to the meanings. Many people can falsely accuse pastors of many things, but false accusations do not take away from the pastor's being *"blameless."*

2. **The Second Biblical Qualification For A Pastor Is That He Is The Husband Of One Wife.**
(1) The first part of this qualification is that a pastor must be a man. The Greek Word for "*husband*" is ANER which means he is a male.
(2) The second part of this qualification is that the pastor must be the "*husband of one wife.*" It is clear that the pastor must be married. No single man or a homosexual man can qualify to be a Scriptural pastor. Another part of this is that he must never be divorced. If he is divorced, he is no longer the "*husband of one wife.*" He is an unmarried man and, if so, he should leave the pastoral ministry. If his wife dies, he is able, after a proper time, to re-marry. When this happens, he would still be the husband of one wife because his first wife has died and is no longer his wife. Death breaks the marriage. Pastors who divorce and re-marry should leave the pastorate. They are not any longer qualified.
3. **The Third Biblical Qualification For A Pastor Is That He Has Faithful Children.**
(1) The first part of this qualification is that a pastor must have children. If he does not have any children, he is not qualified to be a pastor. Having children will enable the pastor to properly help members of his church to deal with their children. Without children, the pastor would have no clue as to how to handle children properly.

THE PASTOR MUST HAVE FAITHFUL CHILDREN
(2) The second part of this qualification is that the pastor's children must be "*faithful.*" They must not be "*accused of riot or unruly.*" This would imply that they were obedient to their parents' guidance and that they are not wayward and worldly while under the pastor's roof. If the pastor does not know how to bring up his children properly, he should not be a pastor.

Titus 1:7

"For a bishop must be blameless, as the steward of God; not selfwilled, not soon angry, not given to wine, no striker, not given to filthy lucre;"

4. **The Fourth Biblical Qualification For A Pastor Is That He Must Be A Steward Of God.**

> **THE MEANING OF THE GREEK WORD, OIKONOMOS**
>
> The Greek Word for "*steward*" is OIKONOMOS. Some of the meanings of that Greek Word are:
>
>> "1. *manager of a household (Lk 12:42; 16:1, 3, 8+);* 2. *administrator, one who has authority and responsibility for something (1Co 4:1, 2; Gal 4:2; Tit 1:7; 1Peter 4:10+);* 3. οἰκονόμος τες πόλεως (oikonomos tēs poleōs), city treasurer (Rom. 16:23)*"

As the steward of God, every pastor must be a blameless and good manager and administrator for the Lord Jesus Christ. He must not be out lf line in any matter either in mundane or moral matters or in things concerning the Words of God and the Bible in general.

5. **The Fifth Biblical Qualification For A Pastor Is That He Must Not Be Selfwilled.**

> **THE MEANING OF THE GREEK WORD, AUTHADES**
>
> The Greek Word for "self-willed" is AUTHADES. Some of the meanings of this Greek Word are:
>
>> "*arrogant, overbearing, as a result of stubbornness, self-will (Tit 1:7; 2Peter 2:10)*"

This would mean that a Biblical pastor must not be arrogant or overbearing as he conducts his ministry in the local church. Sometimes this arrogance is brought on by stubbornness. When a pastor, or any other genuine Christian, is self-willed, arrogant, and stubborn, those who attend his church would not feel right about remaining under his ministry.

6. **The Sixth Biblical Qualification For A Pastor Is That He Must Not Be Soon Angry.**

> **THE MEANING OF THE GREEK WORD, ORGILOS**
>
> The Greek word for "*soon angry*" is ORGILOS. Some of the meanings of that Greek Word are:
>
>> "*angry, inclined to anger; (most versions) quick-tempered; hot tempered (NJB), short-tempered (REB, NEB).*"

Because God wanted to make sure that any Biblical pastor of a local church was not inclined to anger or either quick-tempered; hot tempered; short-tempered, or irritable, He inserted this character trait for pastoral qualifications.

The Lord Jesus Christ was angered against sinful practices when he entered the temple and threw down the moneychangers' tables and said this is a house of God.

- **Matthew 23:27**

"Woe unto you, scribes and Pharisees, hypocrites! for ye are like unto whited sepulchres, which indeed appear beautiful outward, but are within full of dead *men's* bones, and of all uncleanness." And so the Lord Jesus Christ was angry against sin. It is a different type of anger. *"Not soon angry" speaks* about being a hothead who is always being steamed up about something. Proverbs speaks about angry man dangers.

- **Proverbs 22:24**

"Make no friendship with an angry man; and with a furious man thou shalt not go:"
Pastors should be an example and not be an "*angry man*" with whom no one would want to make a friendship.

7. <u>The Seventh Biblical Qualification For A Pastor Is That He Must Not Be Given To Wine</u>.

THE MEANING OF THE GREEK WORD, PAROINOS

The Greek Word for "*given to wine*" is PAROINOS. Some of the meanings of this Greek Word are:

"given to wine, drunken."

The pastor should not even drink wine or any alcoholic beverages in order not to be "given" to them and be "*drunken.*" It is said that by people who are familiar with this situation that some individuals become alcoholic addicts after the first drink.

Here are some verses that use the Greek Word NEPHALIOS. This Greek Word means that every genuine Christian (including the pastors) should abstain from alcohol in any form whatsoever.

> **SEVEN VERSES USING NEPHALIOS**
> **MEANING TOTALLY ABSTAINING FROM ALCOHOL**
>
> 1 Thessalonians 5:6
> ⁶ Therefore let us not sleep, as *do* others; but let us watch and <u>be sober</u>. (KJV)
>
> 1 Thessalonians 5:8
> ⁸ But let us, who are of the day, <u>be sober</u>, putting on the breastplate of faith and love; and for an helmet, the hope of salvation. (KJV)
>
> 1 Timothy 3:2
> ² A bishop then must be blameless, the husband of one wife, <u>vigilant</u>, sober, of good behaviour, given to hospitality, apt to teach; (KJV)
>
> 1 Timothy 3:11
> ¹¹ Even so *must their* wives *be* grave, not slanderers, <u>sober</u>, faithful in all things. (KJV)
>
> 2 Timothy 4:5
> ⁵ But <u>watch thou</u> in all things, endure afflictions, do the work of an evangelist, make full proof of thy ministry. (KJV)
>
> Titus 2:2
> ² That the aged men be <u>sober</u>, grave, temperate, sound in faith, in charity, in patience. (KJV)
>
> 1 Peter 1:13
> ¹³ Wherefore gird up the loins of your mind, <u>be sober</u>, and hope to the end for the grace that is to be brought unto you at the revelation of Jesus Christ; (KJV)

I remember a pastor in Washington state that I used to preach for once a year. I'd go out there and preach. All of a sudden, I understood that he was drinking a little wine at night. He had stomach aches and someone told him to just drink the aches away with wine. When I heard about it, I quoted the above verses that God wants every Christian (especially every pastor) to abstain from alcohol in any form, including wine. Needless to say, I was never invited back to his church any more. Now I'm told that this pastor is not only continuing to drink wine, but is also smoking cigars and a pipe.

8. The Eighth Biblical Qualification For A Pastor Is That He Must Not Be A Striker.

> **THE MEANING OF THE GREEK WORD, PLEKTES**
>
> The Greek Word for *"striker"* is PLEKTES. Some of the meanings of this Greek Word are:
>> *"bully, a violent, pugnacious man (1Tim. 3:3; Titus 1:7)"*

Pastors must not be violent or pugnacious. They must not be a bully. Self-defense is one thing, to prevent a blow coming at you, but a Biblically qualified pastor is not to initiate blows, combat with people, or knock people around. He's to be a testimony to the Lord Jesus Christ, rather than being pugnacious and always ready for fighting, hitting, or smacking somebody. That's not right.

9. The Ninth Biblical Qualification For A Pastor Is That He Must Not Be Given To Filthy Lucre.

> **MEANING OF THE GREEK WORD, AISCHROKERDES**
>
> The Greek Word for *"not given to filthy lucre"* is AISCHROKERDES. Some of the meanings of that Greek Word are:
>> *"shamefully greedy, pursuing dishonest money or possession, eager for base gain, greedy for money (1Ti 3:8; Tit 1:7; 1Ti 3:3 v.r. NA26)"*

"Filthy lucre" is another term for money. Biblically qualified pastors must not be shamefully greedy, eager for base gain, or pursuing dishonest money or possessions. There are many pastors on the TV and the Internet who seem to be guilty of this error. They beg for money and some of them live in million dollar homes. If a pastor is greedy for money, he will not preach on subjects that he knows will cause the wealthy in his congregation to leave his church.

Titus 1:8

"But a lover of hospitality, a lover of good men, sober, just, holy, temperate;"

10. **The Tenth Biblical Qualification For A Pastor Is That He Must Be A Lover Of Hospitality.**

THE MEANING OF THE GREEK WORD, PHILOXENOS

The Greek Word for *"lover of hospitality"* is PHILOXENOS. Some of the meanings of this Greek Word are:

> *"hospitable, pertaining to show care to strangers (1Ti 3:2; Tit 1:8; 1Pe 4:9)"*

A pastor must have a care for fellow Christians who come from other places to visit and have no place to stay. In the times of the New Testament, there were not the many thousands of motels and hotels as there are today. Visiting Christians stayed in the homes of those they were visiting–providing the host was hospitable. This is a requirement of Biblically qualified pastors.

11. **The Eleventh Biblical Qualification For A Pastor Is That He Must Be A Lover Of Good Men.**

MEANING OF THE GREEK WORD, PHILAGATHAOS

The Greek Word For *"lover of good men"* is PHILAGATHOS. Some of the meanings of this Greek Word are:

> *"liking what is good; (most versions)*
> *loving what is good, lover of goodness;*
> *(Titus 1:8)"*

Since the Greek Word is masculine (PHILAGATHOS) it could refer to "good men" as our King James Bible has translated it. A Biblically qualified pastor must love what is good rather than that which is evil, sinful, and wicked. This includes good men rather than evil, sinful, and wicked men.

12. The Twelfth Biblical Qualification For A Pastor Is That He Must Be Sober.

> **THE MEANING OF THE GREEK WORD, SOPHRON**
>
> The Greek Word for *"sober"* is SOPHRON. Some of the meanings of this Greek Word are:
>
> *"1) of a sound mind, sane, in one's senses;*
> *2) curbing one's desires and impulses, self-controlled, temperate"*

A Biblically qualified pastor must be self-controlled and temperate. He cannot be one who is unable to control himself. He cannot be one that might explode in temper tantrums. He must be able to curb his impulses and do that which is pleasing to the Lord Jesus Christ.

13. The Thirteenth Biblical Qualification For A Pastor Is That He Must Be Just.

> **THE MEANING OF THE GREEK WORD, DIKAIOS**
>
> The Greek Word for *"just"* is DIKAIOS. Some of the meanings of this Greek Word are:
>
> *"1) righteous, observing divine laws; 1a) in a wide sense, upright, righteous, virtuous, keeping the commands of God; 1a1) of those who seem to themselves to be righteous, who pride themselves to be righteous, who pride themselves in their virtues, whether real or imagined; 1a2) innocent, faultless, guiltless; 1a3) used of him whose way of thinking, feeling, and acting is wholly conformed to the will of God, and who therefore needs no rectification in the heart or life; 1a3a) only Christ truly: 1a4) approved of or acceptable of God; 1b) in a narrower sense, rendering to each his due and that in a judicial sense, passing just judgment on others, whether expressed in words or shown by the manner of dealing with them."*

A Biblically qualified pastor must be just, righteous, and upright in observing God's Words in the Bible. His church members and other people who know him must see him as just and righteous in his words as well as his actions.

14. The Fourteenth Qualification For A Pastor Is That He Must Be Holy.

> **THE MEANING OF THE GREEK WORD, HOSIOS**
>
> The Greek Word for *"holy"* is HOSIOS. Some of the meanings of this Greek Word are:
>> *"1) undefiled by sin, free from wickedness, religiously observing every moral obligation, pure, holy, pious"*

A Biblically qualified pastor must be undefiled by sin and wickedness. He should be holy and pure. His morality in all areas must be without question. He must be a holy person, not unholy, wicked, or corrupt.

15. The Fifteenth Qualification For A Pastor Is That He Must Be Temperate.

> **THE MEANING OF THE GREEK WORD, ENKRATES**
>
> The Greek Word for *"temperate"* is ENKRATES. Some of the meanings of that Greek Word are:
>> *"1) strong, robust; 2) having power over, possessed of (a thing); 3) mastering, controlling, curbing, restraining; 3a) controlling one's self, temperate, continent."*

A Biblically qualified pastor must have control of himself and able to restrain or curb any wrong or sinful words or actions. He must be in control of his mouth and his actions for the glory of the Lord Jesus Christ Whom he serves.

> **TODAY'S PASTORS MUST MEET ALL 15 STANDARDS**
>
> May God give us many, many pastors who qualify in all fifteen of these standards that the work of our Saviour might go forward with His blessings upon the churches

served by such pastors. Though these fifteen Biblical qualifications are specified for the pastors/bishops/elders, they are also excellent standards for every genuine Christian man, woman, and child to follow as well.

Titus 1:9

"Holding fast the faithful word as he hath been taught, that he may be able by sound doctrine both to exhort and to convince the gainsayers"

1. These Pastors-Bishops-Elders Were Told To *"Hold Fast"* To The Words Of God.

PASTORS MUST HOLD FAST TO GOD'S WORDS

That means that they were not to let the Words of God leave them or slip away from them. They were to hold on to them. There are hundreds, and even thousands of churches today whose churches and pastors are not holding fast to the Words of God.

I was ordained to the gospel ministry in 1953. That's sixty-four years ago. I've seen churches, schools, and many other Christian institutions slip and slide from their former Biblical positions rather than holding them fast. God demands that we hold fast to the words of God.

2. These Pastors-Bishops-Elders Were Told To *"Hold Fast"* To *"Faithful"* Words.

PASTORS MUST HOLD FAST ONLY FAITHFUL WORDS

They were not just to hold fast to all sorts of words, but only to *"faithful Words."* The Words that they hold fast to must be *"faithful."* These must not be the fake and phony scriptures that are founded on the false Hebrew, Aramaic, and Gnostic critical Greek texts on which most of the current Bibles in English and other languages are based.

In English, these false-based versions include the ASV, the NASV, the RSV, the NRSV, the NIV, the ESV and scores of other false English versions. These are not *"faithful"* Words. These new versions contain at least 356 doctrinal passages that contain false doctrines. The King James Bible is based on true Hebrew, Aramaic, and Greek Words which have none of these doctrinal errors.

3. These Pastors-Bishops-Elders Were Told To "*Hold Fast*" To "Faithful" Words As They Were Taught.

Paul taught Pastor Titus the Words and doctrines that he was to "*hold fast.*" This should be practiced by every pastor from the time of Titus to the end of time. Neither Titus, or any other pastors should discard the "*faithful Words*" taught by Paul and other New Testament writers.

4. These Pastors-Bishops-Elders Were Told To "*Hold Fast*" To "Faithful" Words To Make Them Able To Use Sound Doctrine Properly.

The words, "*that he may be able*" are in the Greek present tense. This means that the pastors should be continually and always able, "*by sound doctrine*" to "*exhort and convince the gainsayers.*" Titus and all pastors must have "*sound doctrine*" based upon the sound Words and doctrines of God found in sound Bibles.

With these tools, Titus and other pastors would be able to do two things: (1) "*exhort*" and (2) "*convince.*") I believe "*exhort*" has to do with genuine Christians in order to build them up in the doctrines of the Words of God. I believe the "*convince*" would refer to the "*gainsayers.*"

THE MEANING OF THE GREEK WORD, ANTILEGO

The Greek Word for "*gainsayer*" is ANTILEGO. Some of the meanings of that Greek Word are:

"*1) to speak against, gainsay, contradict;
2) to oppose one's self to one, decline to obey him, declare one's self against him, refuse to have anything to do with him.*"

THE MEANING OF THE GREEK WORD, ELEGCHO

The Greek Word for "*convince*" is ELEGCHO. Some of the meanings of that Greek Word are:

"*1) to convict, refute, confute; 1a) generally with a suggestion of shame of the person convicted; 1b) by conviction to*

> *bring to the light, to expose; 2) to find fault with, correct; 2a) by; 2a1) to reprehend severely, chide, admonish, reprove; 2a2) to call to account, show one his fault, demand an explanation; 2b) by deed; 2b1) to chasten, to punish."*

Titus and other pastors who see those who deny the truths of God's Words, should refute, bring to light, and expose them, reprehending them severely. In addition to preaching and teaching God's Words, our Bible For Today Baptist church seeks to obey this command as well.

Verses On "Hold Fast"

- **Jeremiah 8:5**

"Why *then* is this people of Jerusalem slidden back by a perpetual backsliding? they hold fast deceit, they refuse to return."

That's what we are not to hold fast--deceit or anything that is false.

- **1 Thessalonians 5:21**

"Prove all things; hold fast that which is good."

We are to hold fast the good.

- **2 Timothy 1:13**

"Hold fast the form of sound words, which thou hast heard of me, in faith and love which is in Christ Jesus."

Hold these Words tight. Don't leave them for any preacher, any church, any school, or any other person or group.

- **Hebrews 4:14**

"Seeing then that we have a great high priest, that is passed into the heavens, Jesus the Son of God, let us hold fast *our* profession."

True Christians must hold fast their faithful doctrines of the Bible.

- **Hebrews 10:23**

"Let us hold fast the profession of *our* faith without wavering; (for he *is* faithful that promised;)"

There must be no wavering from holding fast the Biblical doctrines of the faith.

Verses On Faithful
- **Luke 16:10**

"He that is faithful in that which is least is faithful also in much: and he that is unjust in the least is unjust also in much."

Faithfulness is reflected in little things as well as big things.
- **1 Corinthians 4:2**

"Moreover it is required in stewards, that a man be found faithful."

Stewards are people who look after the things of their masters. They must be faithful.
- **2 Timothy 2:2**

"And the things that thou hast heard of me among many witnesses, the same commit thou to faithful men, who shall be able to teach others also."

FAITHFUL WORDS MUST BE PASSED ON

Faithful teachings and doctrines must be given to faithful men who can teach these doctrines to others.

Verses On Sound Doctrine
- **2 Timothy 4:3**

"For the time will come when they will not endure sound doctrine; but after their own lusts shall they heap to themselves teachers, having itching ears;"

MANY TODAY HOLD HERETICAL DOCTRINES

These times have been upon our churches and people for many decades now. There is a refusal on the part of great numbers of people to stand for the sound doctrines of the Bible. They have, instead, given themselves over to heretical doctrines and views.

- **Titus 2:1**

"But speak thou the things which become sound doctrine:"

Sound Bible doctrine should be preached by pastor Titus and by all the other pastors in the world.

Titus 1:10

"For there are many unruly and vain talkers and deceivers, specially they of the circumcision"

Paul told Pastor Timothy that, even in his small island of Crete, there were many unruly and vain deceivers.

THE MEANING OF THE GREEK WORD, ANUPOTAKTOS

The Greek Word for *"unruly"* is ANUPOTAKTOS. Some of the meanings of this Greek Word are:

"1) not made subject, unsubjected; 2) that cannot be subjected to control, disobedient, unruly, refractory."

THE MEANING OF THE GREEK WORD, MATAIOLOGOS

The Greek Word for *"vain talkers"* is: MATAIOLOGOS. Some of the meanings of that Greek Word are:

"1) an idle talker, one who utters empty senseless things"

THE MEANING OF THE GREEK WORD, PHRENAPATES

The Greek Word for *"deceivers"* is: PHRENAPATES. Some of the Meanings of that Greek Word are:

"1) a mind deceiver, a seducer"

There were many who fit into these three categories, especially those who were Jews.

Verses On Unruly

- **1 Thessalonians 5:14**

"Now we exhort you, brethren, <u>warn them that are unruly</u>, comfort the feebleminded, support the weak, be patient toward all *men*."

Unruly people are to be warned. They should follow the rules laid down in the Bible.

- **Titus 1:6**

"If any be blameless, the husband of one wife, having <u>faithful children not accused of riot or unruly</u>."

One of the qualifications of the pastor-bishop-elder is that he should have control of his children, not accused of being unruly.

- **James 3:8**

"But the tongue can no man tame; *it is* an unruly evil, full of deadly poison."

Only true Christians who allow God to control them can tame their unruly tongues.

Verses On Deceivers

- **Matthew 24:4-5**

"And Jesus answered and said unto them, Take heed that no man deceive you. For many shall come in my name, saying, I am Christ; and shall deceive many."

CHRISTIANS MUST NOT DECEIVE OR BE DECEIVED

Paul warns Titus and all genuine Christians about deceiving or being deceived. There are many people (and even pastors in churches) who say that they are Christians, but are not. They're deceivers. Be very careful of deceivers. Don't let anyone deceive you.

- **Matthew 24:11**

"And many false prophets shall rise, and shall deceive many."

False prophets who deceive people are with us today. Genuine Christians must follow the Bible closely so as not to be deceived by anyone.

- **Romans 16:18**

"For they that are such serve not our Lord Jesus Christ, but their own belly; and by good words and fair speeches deceive the hearts of the simple."

Deceivers have their techniques practiced so as to deceive as many people as possible.

- **1 Corinthians 3:18**

"Let no man deceive himself. If any man among you seemeth to be wise in this world, let him become a fool, that he may be wise."

THE DANGERS OF SELF-DECEPTION

Self-deception is very dangerous. When people believe that they are skilled or learned in some area, but really they are not. They deceive themselves and many others as well with their arrogance.

- **1 Corinthians 15:33**

"Be not deceived: evil communications corrupt good manners." The Corinthian Christians were being deceived. This Greek present tense means that they should stop being deceived.

- **Galatians 6:7**

"Be not deceived; God is not mocked: for whatsoever a man soweth, that shall he also reap."

The Christians at Galatia were told to stop being deceived. God knows their hearts and is not fooled or deceived by them.

- **Ephesians 4:14**

"That we *henceforth* be no more children, tossed to and fro, and carried about with every wind of doctrine, by the sleight of men, *and* cunning craftiness, whereby they lie in wait to deceive;"

CHRISTIANS SHOULD NOT BE TOSSED TO AND FRO

Genuine Christians should not be deceived by every wind of new doctrine that churches and others have come up with. Hold fast to Bible doctrine only.

- **Ephesians 5:6a**

"Let no man deceive you with vain words:"

Vain and empty words deceive many, but they should never deceive true Christians.

- **2 Thessalonians 2:3a**

"Let no man deceive you by any means:"

No genuine Christian should be deceived by any means or methods at all.

- **1 Timothy 2:14**

"And Adam was not deceived, but the woman being deceived was in the transgression."

EVE WAS DECEIVED BY THE SATAN-SERPENT

Eve was the one who was deceived by the devil serpent, not Adam, but God holds Adam, as the head of his family, responsible for Eve's action, thus bringing death upon all mankind.

- **2 Timothy 3:13**

"But evil men and seducers shall wax worse and worse, deceiving, and being deceived."

These deceivers have waxed worse and worse unto this very day. They are deceived themselves and deceive others.

- **Titus 3:3**

"For we ourselves also were sometimes foolish, disobedient, deceived, serving divers lusts and pleasures, living in malice and envy, hateful, *and* hating one another."

Paul admits that, before he became a Christian, he was sometimes deceived.

- **1 John 1:8**

"If we say that we have no sin, we deceive ourselves, and the truth is not in us."

Some people say they have no sin. If they say that, they lie and are deceiving themselves.

- **1 John 3:7**

"Little children, let no man deceive you: he that doeth righteousness is righteous, even as he is righteous."

True Christians should not be deceived by anything.

- **2 John 1:7**

"For many deceivers are entered into the world, who confess not that Jesus Christ is come in the flesh. This is a deceiver and an antichrist."

> **ANTICHRISTS DENY CHRIST'S INCARNATION**
>
> Those who deny the incarnation of the Lord Jesus Christ are deceivers and antichrists. This includes thousands of churches of many denominations and their false ministers.

- **Revelation 12:9**

"And the great dragon was cast out, that old serpent, called the Devil, and Satan, which deceiveth the whole world: he was cast out into the earth, and his angels were cast out with him."

Satan is even now deceiving the entire world.

- **Revelation 13:14a**

"And deceiveth them that dwell on the earth by *the means of those miracles* which he had power to do in the sight of the beast;"

One of the methods of deceiving people is by performing false miracles.

- **Revelation 18:23c**

"for by thy sorceries were all nations deceived."

Sorceries will be and are the means by which many people around the world are deceived.

- **Revelation 20:3**

"And cast him into the bottomless pit, and shut him up, and set a seal upon him, that he should deceive the nations no more, till the thousand years should be fulfilled: and after that he must be loosed a little season."

During the millennial reign of the Lord Jesus Christ, Satan will be shut up and unable to deceive the nations until he is loosed. Then he will resume his massive deceptions.

- **Revelation 20:10**

"And the devil that deceived them was cast into the lake of fire and brimstone, where the beast and the false prophet *are*, and shall be tormented day and night for ever and ever."

SATAN WILL BE CAST INTO HELL'S LAKE OF FIRE

At the end of the millennial reign of the Lord Jesus Christ, Satan will be cast into the lake of fire of Hell where the beast and the false prophet are. They will still be suffering the pains of Hell for 1,000 years. It's not as Billy Graham has stated back in the 1950's when stated that there is no fire in Hell. All those who have rejected the Lord Jesus Christ as their Saviour will be *"tormented day and night for ever."*

Titus 1:11

"Whose mouths must be stopped, who subvert whole houses, teaching things which they ought not, for filthy lucre's sake."

Titus is referring to these deceivers and unruly false teachers. The remedy that he recommends is that their *"mouths must be stopped."*

THE MEANING OF THE GREEK WORD, EPISTOMIZO

The Greek Word for *"stopped"* is EPISTOMIZO. Some of the meanings of this Greek Word are:

"*1) to bridle or stop up the mouth; 2) metaph. to stop the mouth, reduce to silence*"

It's true that false teachers' mouths should be silenced, but how to do it is another question. The Lord is able to do it if He desires to.

These unscriptural teachers subvert whole houses in order to make money by teaching things that they should not teach.

> **THE MEANING OF THE GREEK WORD, ANATREPO**
> The Greek Word for *"subvert"* is: ANATREPO. Some of the meanings of this Greek Word are:
> > *"1) to overthrow, overturn, destroy; 2) to subvert"*

These false teachers were possibly invited into houses by people who thought they were sound in the faith. But afterward, their false teachings destroyed the entire house by various heretical doctrines. The verb for *"teaching"* is in the Greek present tense. It indicates that these heretics were continually and perpetually teaching their heresies.

> **FALSE TEACHERS' MOTIVE--FILTHY LUCRE**
> Notice the motivation that these false teachers had. It was *"for filthy lucre's sake."* They wanted to make money. Because of this, they taught the doctrines and teachings that pleased those who sponsored them.

Oftentimes, even in the present time, preachers who preach the straight Bible truths find many of their congregation leaving their church. Truth often offends those who prefer their error.

Titus 1:12-13

"One of themselves, even a prophet of their own, said, The Cretians are alway liars, evil beasts, slow bellies. This witness is true. Wherefore rebuke them sharply, that they may be sound in the faith;"

This prophet who was a witness spoke truly that the Cretians were always liars. Paul told Pastor Titus what to do with these lying false teachers. He was to *"rebuke them sharply."*

> **THE MEANING OF THE GREEK WORD, ELEGCHO**
> The Greek Word for *"rebuke"* is ELEGCHO. Some of the meanings of this Greek Word are:
> > *"1) to convict, refute, confute; 1a) generally with a suggestion of shame of the person convicted; 1b) by conviction to*

> *bring to the light, to expose; 2) to find fault with, correct; 2a) by word; 2a1) to reprehend severely, chide, admonish, reprove; 2a2) to call to account, show one his fault, demand an explanation; 2b) by deed; 2b1) to chasten, to punish."*

The *"rebuke"* was not simply with some kind and generous words. Their heretical teachings had to be rebuked *"sharply."*

THE MEANING OF THE GREEK WORD, APOTOMOS

The Greek Word for *"sharply"* is APOTOMOS. Some of the meanings of this Greek Word are:

"1) abruptly, precipitously; 2) sharply, severely, curtly"

This rebuke was not to be just with a light tap against such false teaching, but it was to be done abruptly. It should not be put off. It was to be done sharply and severely. This is what Pastor Titus and faithful pastors today should do with all false doctrines that they might confront.

Quite often, these false teachers today put many of their false teachings either on audio or video tapes or in books or pamphlets. I rebuke such teachings sharply when I find them.

- **1 Timothy 5:20**

"Them that sin rebuke before all, that others also may fear."
The people referred to in this verse are pastors-bishops-elders that sin. Based on the testimony of two or three honest and informed witnesses about these leaders' sins, they should be rebuked before all people lest others might be tempted to sin in the same manner. It should not be kept secret or concealed.

- **2 Timothy 4:2**

"Preach the word; be instant in season, out of season; reprove, rebuke, exhort with all longsuffering and doctrine."
Not only was a pastor of past years and today to *"preach the Words"* of God, but he was also to *"rebuke"* where needed. This was to be done with *"longsuffering and doctrine."*

- **Titus 2:15**

"These things speak, and exhort, and rebuke with all authority. Let no man despise thee."

Titus Expounded Verse by Verse

> **PASTOR TITUS WAS TO REBUKE WITH AUTHORITY**
>
> Pastor Titus was told by Paul to not only speak and exhort, but also to *"rebuke with all authority"* when needed. It is an authority given to Bible-preaching and teachings pastors to *"rebuke"* when necessary and needed. Like everything else pastors are to do, it should be done with wisdom.

Verses On "The Faith" And Doctrine

It should be noted that when the Greek Word for *"faith"* is preceded by the Greek definite article, it refers to the doctrines and teachings of the Bible.

- **2 Timothy 4:3**

  "For the time will come when they will not endure sound doctrine; but after their own lusts shall they heap to themselves teachers, having itching ears;"

Paul reminded Pastor Timothy that there will come a time when people would not endure *"sound doctrine,"* but would gather to themselves those who teach unscriptural and false doctrines.

- **Titus 1:9**

  "Holding fast the faithful word as he hath been taught, that he may be able by sound doctrine both to exhort and to convince the gainsayers."

As mentioned earlier in this chapter, sound doctrine can exhort the genuine Christians and rebuke the unbelievers.

- **Titus 2:1-2**

  "But speak thou the things which become sound doctrine: That the aged men be sober, grave, temperate, sound in faith, in charity, in patience."

Pastor Titus was urged by the Apostle Paul to speak things that fit in with sound doctrine.

- **Acts 6:7**

  "And the word of God increased; and the number of the disciples multiplied in Jerusalem greatly; and a great company of the priests were obedient to the faith."

The many true Christians who were apostles and priests were said to be *"obedient to the faith."* **When the Greek Word for "faith" has the Greek article before it, as in this verse, it refers to the doctrines of the faith.**

- **Acts 16:5**

  "And so were the churches <u>established in the faith</u>, and increased in number daily."

These churches were established and grounded in the doctrines of the faith and increased in number daily. We need such churches today as well.

- **Romans 1:5**

  "By whom we have received grace and apostleship, for <u>obedience to the faith</u> among all nations, for his name:"

God wants every true Christian today to be obedient to the doctrinal faith of the Bible.

- **1 Corinthians 16:13**

  "Watch ye, <u>stand fast in the faith</u>, quit you like men, be strong."

KNOW DOCTRINE AND STAND FAST IN IT

Genuine Christians must be determined first to know the doctrines of the Bible faith, and next to stand fast in them and never change them!

- **Colossians 2:7**

  "Rooted and built up in him, and <u>stablished in the faith</u>, as ye have been taught, <u>abounding therein</u> with thanksgiving."

God wants true Christians to be firmly planted, fixed, and established in the doctrinal Bible faith without any wavering or drifting.

- **1 Timothy 3:13**

  "For they that have used the office of a deacon well purchase to themselves a good degree, and <u>great boldness in the faith which is in Christ Jesus</u>."

Paul urged Pastor Timothy to be certain that those who are chosen to be deacons in their local churches must have great boldness in the Biblical doctrines of the faith given to us by the Lord Jesus Christ.

- **1 Timothy 4:1**

  "Now the Spirit speaketh expressly, that in the latter times <u>some shall depart from the faith</u>, giving heed to seducing spirits, and doctrines of devils;"

This verse has come to pass in this year of 2017 and all around the world where thousands and thousands of churches have departed from Biblical faith. It is a very sad situation!

- **2 Timothy 4:7**

  "I have fought a good fight, I have finished *my* course, <u>I have kept the faith</u>:"

All through his life, Paul guarded the Biblical faith. It is very unsettling to see this doctrinal faith shattered in so many different ways.
- **Jude 1:3**
"Beloved, when I gave all diligence to write unto you of the common salvation, it was needful for me to write unto you, and exhort *you* that ye should earnestly contend for the faith which was once delivered unto the saints."

> **OUR CHURCH CONTENDS EARNESTLY FOR THE DOCTRINES OF THE FAITH**
>
> That's what our Bible For Today Baptist Church seeks to do in all of its services. It is for the Biblical faith which was once delivered that we earnestly contend. It must be the doctrinal faith that was "once delivered to the saints" for which genuine Christians must contend. This is why Christians must contend for the preserved Hebrew, Aramaic, and Greek Words and accurate translations of these Words such as the King James Bible. Other modern versions have forsaken the preserved Hebrew, Aramaic, and Greek Words as their basis and have very inaccurately translated these improper original Words. This is why our Bible For Today ministries and our Dean Burgon Society write so many articles, pamphlets, and books that *"earnestly contend for the faith which was once delivered unto the saints."*

Titus 1:14

"Not giving heed to Jewish fables, and commandments of men, that turn from the truth;"

There are all kinds of commandments of men that people are hearing today. They come from the Roman Catholic church that puts the commandments of their Pope and church leaders above the Bible. They come from apostate Protestant church leaders like Bill Hybels, Rick Warren, Joel Osteen, and many others. They come from the heretical world religions. Sometimes they even come from compromising Bible-believing church leaders.

What happens when people give heed to these unscriptural commandments of men? Those receiving them are turned from the

Words and commands of the Bible. Genuine Christians must stick to the Words of God, no matter what others might say. Genuine Christians should cling to Biblical truths without wavering. The Bible is clear about the sin of homosexuality, both male and female, bestiality, polygamy and many other sinful practices commended by many in our day.

Titus 1:15

"Unto the pure all things are pure: but unto them that are defiled and unbelieving is nothing pure; but even their mind and conscience is defiled;"

I believe this means that those who are true Christians do not dabble in impurities, but only in pure things.

THE MEANING OF THE GREEK WORD, KATHAROS

The Greek Word for *"pure"* is KATHAROS. Some of the meanings of that Greek Word are:

"1) clean, pure; 1a) physically; 1a1) purified by fire; 1a2) in a similitude, like a vine cleansed by pruning and so fitted to bear fruit; 1b) in a levitical sense; 1b1) clean, the use of which is not forbidden, imparts no uncleanness; 1c) ethically; 1c1) free from corrupt desire, from sin and guilt; 1c2) free from every admixture of what is false, sincere genuine; 1c3) blameless, innocent; 1c4) unstained with the guilt of anything"

Genuine Christians should not be entangling themselves with impurities of any kind. They should keep their thoughts, minds, and bodies pure by diligently following the written Words of God in the Bible.

Verses On Pure

- **Matthew 5:8**

"<u>Blessed *are* the pure in heart</u>: for they shall see God."

Though this is not easy in these impure and filthy days we are living in, God wants true Christians' hearts to be pure.

- **Philippians 4:8**
  "Finally, brethren, whatsoever things are true, whatsoever things *are* honest, whatsoever things *are* just, whatsoever things *are* pure, whatsoever things *are* lovely, whatsoever things *are* of good report; if *there be* any virtue, and if *there be* any praise, think on these things."

Genuine Christians are told to think on "pure" things.

- **1 Timothy 1:5**
  "Now the end of the commandment is charity out of a pure heart, and *of* a good conscience, and *of* faith unfeigned:"

Love should be out of a pure heart, not out of pretense.

- **1 Timothy 3:9**
  "Holding the mystery of the faith in a pure conscience."

Pastor Timothy was told by Paul to have a pure conscience which would not be defiled by any impurity.

- **1 Timothy 5:22**
  "Lay hands suddenly on no man, neither be partaker of other men's sins: keep thyself pure."

PASTOR TIMOTHY WAS TO KEEP HIMSELF PURE

Paul told Pastor Timothy to keep himself pure. This includes the thoughts as well as the actions. It is not an easy thing to do with the strong power of the sinful flesh fighting such purity. God had to help him in his battle of self control.

- **2 Timothy 1:3**
  "I thank God, whom I serve from *my* forefathers with pure conscience, that without ceasing I have remembrance of thee in my prayers night and day;"

Paul repeated his use of the pure conscience from 1 Timothy 3:9. Even in Paul's second Roman imprisonment he served God with a pure and undefiled conscience.

- **2 Timothy 2:22**
  "Flee also youthful lusts: but follow righteousness, faith, charity, peace, with them that call on the Lord out of a pure heart."

Youthful lusts might start in the youth, but they can be enacted at any age. True Christians must call upon the Lord to help them keep their hearts pure.

- **1 Peter 1:22**
"Seeing ye have purified your souls in obeying the truth through the Spirit unto unfeigned love of the brethren, *see that ye* love one another with a pure heart fervently:"

Genuine Christians are commanded to love one another with a pure heart fervently, even though they might differ with one another on some doctrines or practices.

- **2 Peter 3:1**
"This second epistle, beloved, I now write unto you; in *both* which I stir up your pure minds by way of remembrance:"

True Christians' pure minds must be stirred up to remember the Words and promises of God.

Titus 1:16

"They profess that they know God; but in works they deny him, being abominable, and disobedient, and unto every good work reprobate."

The people Paul told Titus to *"rebuke sharply"* (v. 13) are described here. These Cretians should be rebuked sharply for a number of things.

THE CRETANS WERE TO BE REBUKED

1. Their Profession Is Denied By Their Works. In this case, they are really lying and should be rebuked for such behavior

2. They Are Abominable And Disobedient. When genuine Christians looked at the actions of these Cretians they could see clearly that they were both *"abominable"* as well as *"disobedient."*

3. All Their Works Are Reprobate.

THE MEANING OF THE GREEK WORD, ADOKIMOS

The Greek Word for *"reprobate"* is ADOKIMOS. Some of the meanings of that Greek Word are:

"1) not standing the test, not approved; 1a) properly used of metals and coins; 2) that which does not prove itself such as it ought; 2a) unfit for, unproved, spurious, reprobate."

With all of these sins listed against these Cretians, it is no wonder that the Apostle Paul urged Pastor Titus to *"rebuke them sharply."* May all true Christians keep away from these evil works and live honestly and constantly to please the Lord Jesus Christ.

Titus Chapter Two

Titus 2:1

"But speak thou the things which become sound doctrine:"

The Greek Word for *"speak"* refers to the preaching that Titus is to do. <u>The Greek Word for *"speak"* is in the Greek present tense which shows that he is always and continue to preach things that become sound doctrine.</u> Paul does not want Titus ever to preach false doctrine. He must follow the Bible's teachings as he preaches to his congregation in Crete and to others as well.

> **THE MEANING OF THE GREEK WORD, PREPO**
>
> The Greek Word for *"become"* is PREPO. Some of the meanings of that Greek Word are:
>
> *"1) to stand out, to be conspicuous, to be eminent; 2) to be becoming, seemly, fit."*

The things that Titus was to preach should stand out clearly and fit the needs that people have.

> **THE MEANING OF THE GREEK WORD, HUGIAINO**
>
> The Greek Word for *"sound"* is HUGIAINO. Some of the meanings of that Greek Word are:
>
> *"1) to be sound, to be well, to be in good health; 2) metaphor--2a) of Christians whose opinions are free from any mixture of error 2b) of one who keeps the graces and is strong."*

Titus must be sure to preach healthy doctrines that are free from any mixture of error. Many pastors, for one reason or other, all around the world, fail to heed this valuable exhortation.

Verses On Doctrine

- **Matthew 16:12**

"Then understood they how that he bade *them* not beware of the leaven of bread, but of the doctrine of the Pharisees and of the Sadducees."

The Lord Jesus Christ told His followers to beware of the false doctrines of both the Pharisees and the Sadducees.

- **Mark 1:22**

"And they were astonished at his doctrine: for he taught them as one that had authority, and not as the scribes."

The hearers of the Lord Jesus Christ were astonished at His doctrines. He taught with authority, as the scribes.

- **John 7:16**

"Jesus answered them, and said, My doctrine is not mine, but his that sent me."

All the teachings of the Lord Jesus Christ were those in line with God the Father's teachings as well.

- **Acts 2:42**

"And they continued stedfastly in the apostles' doctrine and fellowship, and in breaking of bread, and in prayers."

THE EARLY CHURCH KEPT THE PROPER DOCTRINES

The early church leaders didn't depart from the apostles' doctrine which was based on the teachings of the Words of God. Sad to say, many of the modern day churches have seriously departed from the doctrines of God's Words.

- **Romans 16:17**

"Now I beseech you, brethren, mark them which cause divisions and offences contrary to the doctrine which ye have learned; and avoid them."

Paul ordered the genuine Christians at Rome to identify clearly those people who hold positions contrary to the Bible's doctrine, and avoid them and separate from them. This should be practiced today as well.

- **Ephesians 4:14**

"That we *henceforth* be no more children, tossed to and fro, and carried about with every wind of doctrine, by the sleight of men, *and* cunning craftiness, whereby they lie in wait to deceive;"

Many professing Christians and pastors today are tossed to and fro with every wind of false doctrines.
- **1 Timothy 4:6**

"If thou put the brethren in remembrance of these things, thou shalt be a good minister of Jesus Christ, <u>nourished up in the words of faith and of good doctrine</u>, whereunto thou hast attained."

The only thing that can nourish genuine Christians is good doctrine found in the Words of God.
- **1 Timothy 4:13**

"Till I come, <u>give attendance</u> to reading, to exhortation, <u>to doctrine</u>."

Attention and heed should be given by all true Christians to the doctrines and teachings of God's Words.
- **1 Timothy 4:16**

"<u>Take heed</u> unto thyself, and <u>unto the doctrine</u>; continue in them: for in doing this thou shalt both save thyself, and them that hear thee."

It is not enough to know doctrine. It must be heeded and continued in order to be profited by it.
- **1 Timothy 5:17**

"Let the elders that rule well be counted worthy of double honour, especially <u>they who labour in the word and doctrine</u>."

The pastors/bishops/elders who labor in the Words of God and doctrine are worthy of double honor.
- **2 Timothy 3:16-17**

"<u>All scripture</u> *is* given by inspiration of God, and <u>is profitable for doctrine</u>, for reproof, for correction, for instruction in righteousness: That the man of God may be perfect, throughly furnished unto all good works."

One of the things that Scripture is profitable for is doctrine. Doctrine is the teachings and theology of God's Words in the Bible.
- **2 Timothy 4:2**

"Preach the word; be instant in season, out of season; <u>reprove, rebuke, exhort with all longsuffering and doctrine</u>."

> **PASTORS MUST REPROVE WITH LONGSUFFERING**
> All reproving, rebuking, and exhorting of a pastor must be both with longsuffering and also with doctrine. It must line up with Biblical truth.

- **2 John 1:9**
"Whosoever transgresseth, and abideth not in the doctrine of Christ, hath not God. He that abideth in the doctrine of Christ, he hath both the Father and the Son."

To be in fellowship with both God the Father and God the Son, genuine Christians must follow and abide in the doctrines and teachings concerning the Lord Jesus Christ.

- **2 John 1:10-11**
"If there come any unto you, and bring not this doctrine, receive him not into *your* house, neither bid him God speed: For he that biddeth him God speed is partaker of his evil deeds."

> **DON'T ADMIT FALSE TEACHERS INTO YOUR HOUSE**
> Those bringing false doctrines should not be admitted into any one's house, nor should they be bidden "*God speed.*" This includes Jehovah's Witnesses or any other false cult. If you let them inside, they may convert you, your children, or others in your family.

Four Verses On Sound Doctrine

- **1 Timothy 1:10**
"For whoremongers, for them that defile themselves with mankind, for menstealers, for liars, for perjured persons, and if there be any other thing that is contrary to sound doctrine;"

The law was made (according to verse 9) for all these sins that are contrary to sound and healthy doctrine.

- **2 Timothy 4:3**
"For the time will come when they will not endure sound doctrine; but after their own lusts shall they heap to themselves teachers, having itching ears;"

That time spoken of in this verse has been true for many decades now. It is still true in our days as well. It is a sad and dangerous thing to reject the Bible's "*sound doctrine.*"

- **Titus 1:9**
"Holding fast the faithful word as he hath been taught, that <u>he may be able by sound doctrine both to exhort and to convince the gainsayers</u>."
"*Sound doctrine*" gave Pastor Titus the ability to exhort the true Christians and convict the unbelievers.
- **Titus 2:1**
"But <u>speak thou the things which become sound doctrine</u>:"
Just as Pastor Titus was to preach the things that are fitting to sound doctrine, so pastors today must do the same.

Titus 2:2

"That the aged men be sober, grave, temperate, sound in faith, in charity, in patience."

Titus is to speak to his congregation about qualities that go along with sound doctrine. In the coming verses, Paul mentions a total of eighteen qualities that should accompany such sound doctrine. Of these eighteen qualities, there are six expected from the aged men and twelve expected for aged women.

Six Things For Aged Men That Are In Line With Sound Doctrine

Paul tells Pastor Titus that he should preach that the aged men should have six different qualities in their lives. I believe it will be sufficient, in most cases, just to give the six Greek Words used and some of their meanings for these six qualities needed for the aged men.

1. <u>Aged Men Should Be Sober.</u>

THE MEANING OF THE GREEK WORD, NEPHALEOS

The Greek Word for "*sober*" is NEPHALEOS. Some of the meanings of that Greek Word are:

"*1) sober, temperate; 1a) abstaining from wine, either entirely or at least from its immoderate use; 1b) of things free from all wine, as vessels, offerings.*"

I believe that the best meaning of that Greek Word is to completely abstain from wine or any alcoholic drink. It is inappropriate for these aged men to abuse their bodies with the drinking of alcohol.

2. Aged Men Should Be Grave.

> **THE MEANING OF THE GREEK WORD, SEMNOS**
>
> The Greek Word for "*grave*" is SEMNOS. Some of the meanings of this Greek Word are:
>
>> "*1) August, venerable, reverend; 2) to be venerated for character, honourable; 2a) of persons; 2b) of deeds.*"

3. Aged Men Should Be Temperate.

> **THE MEANING OF THE GREEK WORD, SOPHRON**
>
> The Greek Word for "*temperate*" is SOPHRON. Some of the meanings of this Greek Word are:
>
>> "*1) of a sound mind, sane, in one's senses; 2) curbing one's desires and impulses, self-controlled, temperate.*"

4. Aged Men Should Be Sound In The Faith.

> **THE MEANING OF THE GREEK WORD, HUGIAINO**
>
> The Greek Word for "*sound*" is HUGIANO. Some of the meanings of this Greek Word are:
>
>> "*1) to be sound, to be well, to be in good health; 2) metaph. 2a) of Christians whose opinions are free from any mixture of error; 2b) of one who keeps the graces and is strong.*"

The Greek Word for "*sound*" is in the Greek present tense which indicates a continuing need to have such soundness in the faith.

> **THE MEANING OF THE GREEK WORD, PISTIS**
>
> The Greek Word for "*faith*" is PISTIS. Some of the meanings of this Greek Word are:
>
>> "*1) conviction of the truth of anything, belief; in the NT of a conviction or belief respecting man's relationship to God and divine things, generally with the included idea of trust and holy fervour born of faith and joined with it 1a) relating to God; 1a1) the conviction that*

> *God exists and is the creator and ruler of all things, the provider and bestower of eternal salvation through Christ; 1b) relating to Christ   1b1) a strong and welcome conviction or belief that Jesus is the Messiah, through whom we obtain eternal salvation in the kingdom of God; 1c) the religious beliefs of Christians; 1d) belief with the predominate idea of trust (or confidence) whether in God or in Christ, springing from faith in the same; 2) fidelity, faithfulness;   2a) the character of one who can be relied on."*

Another thing that should be brought out is that the Greek Word for "*faith*" is preceded by the Greek definite article. This means that "*the faith*" is a reference to the entire body of Biblical teachings and doctrines.

5. **Aged Men Should Be Sound In Charity.**

THE MEANING OF THE GREEK WORD, AGAPE

The Greek Word for "*charity*" is AGAPE. Some of the meanings of this Greek Word are:

> "*1) brotherly love, affection, good will, love, benevolence; 2) love feasts.*"

This love should be sound and genuine. There should not be any fake or phony love on the part of these "*aged men.*"

6. **Aged Men Should Be Sound In Patience.**

THE MEANING OF THE GREEK WORD, HUPOMENE

The Greek Word for "*patience*" is HUPOMENE. Some of the meanings of this Greek Word are:

> "*1) steadfastness, constancy, endurance; 1a) in the NT the characteristic of a man who is not swerved from his deliberate purpose and his loyalty to faith and piety*

> by even the greatest trials and sufferings; 1b) patiently, and steadfastly; 2) a patient, steadfast waiting for; 3) a patient enduring, sustaining, perseverance."

Titus 2:3

"The aged women likewise, that they be in behaviour as becometh holiness, not false accusers, not given to much wine, teachers of good things;"

As mentioned in the preceding verse, there were six qualities expected which Paul wanted Pastor Titus to encourage for the aged men. In the next chapters, there were twelve qualities that Pastor Titus was to encourage for the aged women.

Twelve Things For Aged Women That Are In Line With Sound Doctrine

We're not told what "*aged*" implies. It might be those of age 50, 60, 70, or above. We're not told.

1. Aged Women Should Have Holy Behavior.

THE MEANING OF THE GREEK WORD, HIEROPREPES

The Greek Word for "*holiness*" is HIEROPREPES. Some of the meanings for that Greek Word are:

> "1) befitting men, places, actions or sacred things to God; 2) reverent."

2. Aged Women Should Not Be False Accusers.

THE MEANING OF THE GREEK WORD, DIABOLOS

The Greek Word for "*false accuser*" is DIABOLOS. Some of the meanings of this Greek Word are:

> "1) prone to slander, slanderous, accusing falsely; 1a) a calumniator, false accuser, slanderer; 2) metaph. applied to a man who, by opposing the cause of God may be

> *said to act the part of the devil or to side with him; Satan the prince of the demons, the author of evil, persecuting good men, estranging mankind from God and enticing them to sin, afflicting them with diseases by means of demons who take possession of their bodies at his bidding."*

3. <u>Aged Women Should Not Be Given To Much Wine.</u>

THE MEANING OF THE GREEK WORD, DOULOO

The Greek Word for *"given"* is DOULOO. Some of the meanings of this Greek Word are:

> *"1) to make a slave of, reduce to bondage; 2) metaph. give myself wholly to one's needs and service; make myself a bondman to him."*

These aged women should not be **enslaved** to much wine. Some have said that after the first drink of alcoholic beverages, many people become addicted to alcohol. If this is true, to please God, genuine Christian aged men (or women, or children of any age) should not even take that first drink lest they might become alcoholics after that first drink.

4. <u>Aged Women Should Be Teachers Of Good Things.</u>

MEANING OF THE GREEK WORD, KALODIDASKALOS

The Greek Word for *"teachers of good things"* is KALODIDASKALOS. Some of the meanings for this Greek Word are:

> *"1) teaching that which is good, a teacher of goodness."*

This compound Greek Word implies two things: (1) they were able to teach others; (2) they were to teach good things. The source and definition of *"good things"* is the Bible. It is not in the writings of human beings.

Titus 2:4

"That they may teach the young women to be sober, to love their husbands, to love their children,"

In this verse, there is a continuation of the qualities that aged women should have.

5. <u>Aged Women Should Teach The Young Women To Be Sober.</u>

> **THE MEANING OF THE GREEK WORD, SOPHRONIZO**
>
> The Greek Word for "*sober*" is SOPHRONIZO. Some of the meanings of this Greek Word are:
>
> *"1) restore one to his senses; 2) to moderate, control, curb, disciple; 3) to hold one to his duty; 4) to admonish, to exhort earnestly."*

6. <u>Aged Women Should Teach The Young Women To Love Their Husbands.</u>

> **THE MEANING OF THE GREEK WORD, PHILANDROS**
>
> The Greek Word for "love their husbands" is PHILANDROS. One of the meanings of this Greek Word is:
>
> *"1) loving her husband."*

My wife used to teach many classes to various wives. She called these classes ***Husband-Loving Lessons***. These lessons are found in a 291-page book by that title. It is **BFT #3488** if you want to order it. These classes were appreciated by the many ladies who attended.

The above Greek Word that ends in "ANDROS" means a "*male.*" There is no justification of any kind anywhere in the Bible for female or male homosexual marriages or unions. It's a clear Biblical principal for a woman (GUNE) "female" to marry and love her own husband (ANER) "male." Once again, all homosexual marriages are a sin against God.

7. <u>Aged Women Should Teach The Young Women To Love Their Children.</u>

> **THE MEANING OF THE GREEK WORD, PHILOTEKNOS**
> The Greek Word for loving children is PHILOTEKNOS. One of the meanings of this Greek Word is:
> *"1) loving one's offspring or children."*

This is another quality that aged women should possess. <u>If they love children, they certainly would not teach young women to kill their children by abortion</u>. Though children do not always do lovable things, young women should love them anyway. <u>This love includes discipline of the children (1) when they need it; (2) always when they need it; and (3) in a Biblical and proper manner.</u>

Titus 2:5

"To be discreet, chaste, keepers at home, good, obedient to their own husbands, that the word of God be not blasphemed."

Here are some more qualities that aged Christian women are to teach the younger women.

8. <u>Aged Women Should Teach The Young Women To Be Discreet.</u>

> **THE MEANING OF THE GREEK WORD, SOPHRON**
> The Greek Word for *"discreet"* is SOPHRON. Some of the meanings of this Greek Word are:
> *"1) of a sound mind, sane, in one's senses;*
> *2) curbing one's desires and impulses, self-controlled, temperate."*

9. <u>Aged Women Should Teach The Young Women To Be Chaste.</u>

> **THE MEANING OF THE GREEK WORD, HAGNOS**
> The Greek Word for *"chaste"* is HAGNOS. Some of the meanings of that Greek Word are:
> *"1) exciting reverence, venerable, sacred;*
> *2) pure; 2a) pure from carnality, chaste, modest; 2b) pure from every fault, immaculate; 2c) clean."*

They are to be sexually pure, not impure. I was reading one day about the Gnostic religion which was founded in Alexandria, Egypt. This city was where the false Vatican and Sinai manuscripts were constructed. These impure false words form the basis of the false Bible versions in English and the other languages of the world.

THE GNOSTICS ACCEPTED MANY SEXUAL SINS

One of the perverse Gnostic teachings was that fornication and prostitution were acceptable to them. They did not believe in the chastity and sexual purity of both their younger and their older women.

10. Aged Women Should Teach The Young Women To Be Keepers At Home.

THE MEANING OF THE GREEK WORD, OIKOUROS

The Greek Word for "*keepers at home*" is OIKOUROS. Some of the meanings of this Greek Word are:

"1) caring for the house, working at home; 1a) the (watch or) keeper of the house; 1b) keeping at home and taking care of household affairs; 1c) a domestic."

It is true that some houses are easier to care for than others, but these younger women were to be taught by the aged women to take care of their homes and their household affairs. Perhaps some of the young women in Crete were doing other things and neglecting caring for their home.

11. Aged Women Should Teach The Young Women To Be Good.

THE MEANING OF THE GREEK WORD, AGATHOS

The Greek Word for "*good*" is AGATHOS. Some of the meanings of this Greek Word are:

"1) of good constitution or nature; 2) useful, salutary; 3) good, pleasant, agreeable, joyful, happy; 4) excellent, distinguished; 5) upright, honourable."

This Greek Word is stronger than the Word, KALOS. AGAPE is the Greek Word used of God's "*love*" for the entire world in John 3:16:

*"For God so **loved** the world, that he gave his only begotten Son, that whosoever believeth in him should not perish, but have everlasting life."*

12. Aged Women Should Teach The Young Women To Be Obedient To Their Own Husbands.

THE MEANING OF THE GREEK WORD, HUPOTASSO

The Greek Word for *"obedient"* is HUPOTASSO. Some of the meanings of this Greek Word are:

> *"1) to arrange under, to subordinate; 2) to subject, put in subjection; 3) to subject one's self, obey; 4) to submit to one's control; 5) to yield to one's admonition or advice; 6) to obey, be subject; It is also a Greek military term meaning "to arrange [troop divisions] in a military fashion under the command of a leader". In non-military use, it was 'a voluntary attitude of giving in, cooperating, assuming responsibility, and carrying a burden.'"*

This Greek Word for *"obey"* is in the Greek present tense. As such, it is stressed that this obedience is to be continuous rather than just once in a while.

This last instruction for these younger women was so the Word of God would not be blasphemed because of their disobedience to their own husbands.

Titus 2:6

"Young men likewise exhort to be sober minded."

The Apostle Paul told Pastor Titus what he should exhort to the Christian young men in his church.

Young Christian Men Should Be Sober Minded.

THE MEANING OF THE GREEK WORD, SOPHRONEO

The Greek Word for *"sober minded"* is SOPHRONEO. Some of the meanings of this Greek Word are:

> "1) to be of sound mind; 1a) to be in one's right mind; 1b) to exercise self control; 1b1) to put a moderate estimate upon one's self, think of one's self soberly; 1b2) to curb one's passions."

This would be a great thing if all the true Christian young men would possess this quality in their lives. This is the standard that the Apostle Paul told Pastor Titus to exhort the young men about.

Titus 2:7

"In all things shewing thyself a pattern of good works: in doctrine shewing uncorruptness, gravity, sincerity."

Paul also had some specific qualities that Pastor Titus should have in his life as the pastor of the church at Crete.

1. **Pastor Titus Should Be A Pattern Of Good Works.**

THE MEANING OF THE GREEK WORD, TUPOS

The Greek Word for *"pattern"* is TUPOS. Some of the meanings of that Greek Word are:

> "1) the mark of a stroke or blow, print; 2) a figure formed by a blow or impression 2a) of a figure or image; 2b) of the image of the gods; 3) form; 3a) the teaching which embodies the sum and substance of religion and represents it to the mind, manner of writing, the contents and form of a letter; 4) an example; 4a) in the technical sense, the pattern in conformity to which a thing must be made; 4b) in an ethical sense, a dissuasive example, a pattern of warning; 4b1) of ruinous events which serve as admonitions or warnings to others; 4c) an example to be imitated; 4c1) of men worthy of imitation; 4d) in a doctrinal sense; 4d1) of a type i.e. a person or thing prefiguring a future; (Messianic) person or thing."

This Greek Word has a number of very clear meanings of this Word. If Pastor Titus was to be successful in his church on the island of Crete, a number of things should be true in his life. The first thing that Pastor Titus should be is a pattern and an example of good works. Those in his congregation should be able to see good works for the Lord Jesus Christ in his life that would be an example and pattern for them to follow.

2. Pastor Titus Should Have Uncorrupt Bible Doctrine.

THE MEANING OF THE GREEK WORD, ADIAPHTHORIA

The Greek Word for *"uncorruptness"* is ADIAPHTHORIA. Some of the meanings of this Greek Word are:

"1) incorruptibility, soundness, integrity;
1a) of mind."

This soundness and integrity must be practiced in the *"doctrine"* of the Bible.

THE MEANING OF THE GREEK WORD, DIDASKALIA

The Greek Word For *"doctrine"* is DIDASKALIA. Some of the meanings of this Greek Word are:

"1) teaching, instruction; 2) teaching; 2a) that which is taught, doctrine; 2b) teachings, precepts."

Pastor Titus was to be a good pattern and example of sound teachings and instruction of the Bible. This is necessary for all genuine Christian pastors around the world in our day as well.

To do this, these pastors must be aware of the heretical and false Gnostic Critical Greek words in the New Testament and all the heretical and false Bible versions found in all countries of the world that are based upon these heretical Greek words.

GNOSTIC GREEK TEXT DOCTRINAL PERVERSIONS

These pastors should know that there are over 8,000 differences between the Traditional Greek Text and these false Gnostic and Critical Greek Texts. They contain at least 356 doctrinal passages that change many Biblical truths.

Pastor Titus and the pastors of our day must know God's Words from daily study of the Bible so they can be examples of sound Bible preaching to their congregations.

3. **Pastor Titus Should Show Gravity.**

> **THE MEANING OF THE GREEK WORD, SEMNOTES**
>
> The Greek Word for *"gravity"* is SEMNOTES. Some of the meanings of that Greek Word are:
>
> *"1) the characteristic of a thing or person which entitles to reverence and respect, dignity, majesty, sanctity; 2) honour, purity."*

Pastor Timothy and pastors today should show respect, dignity, sanctity, honor, and purity in their lives and ministries.

4. **Pastor Titus Should Show Sincerity.**

> **THE MEANING OF THE GREEK WORD, APHTHARSIA**
>
> The Greek Word for *"sincerity"* is APHTHARSIA. Some of the meanings of this Greek Word are:
>
> *"1) incorruption, perpetuity; 2) purity, sincerity, incorrupt."*

Pastor Titus, and all present-day pastors must evidence purity and sincerity in their public and private ministries.

Titus 2:8

"Sound speech, that cannot be condemned; that he that is of the contrary part may be ashamed, having no evil thing to say of you."

5. **Pastor Titus Should Have Sound Speech That Can't Be Condemned.**

> **THE MEANING OF THE GREEK WORD, HUGIES**
>
> The Greek Word for *"sound"* is HUGIES. Some of the meanings of that Greek Word are:
>
> *"1) sound; 1a) of a man who is sound in body; 2) to make one whole i.e. restore him to health; 3) metaph. teaching which does not deviate from the truth."*

If Pastor Titus's speech is *"sound,"* it does not deviate from the truth. It should be such that the unbelievers, though they don't agree with it, cannot honestly find fault with the truth and propriety of such speech.

6. Pastor Titus Should Live So The Unbelievers Have No Evil Thing To Say About Him.

> **THE MEANING OF THE GREEK WORD, PHAULOS**
> The Greek Word for *"evil"* is PHAULOS. Some of the meanings of this Greek Word are:
> > *"1) easy, slight, ordinary, mean, worthless, of no account; 2) ethically, bad, base, wicked."*

Pastor Titus and all pastors today should live lives so Biblical and sound that those who are lost and unsaved people cannot find any evil or wicked things in their lives.

Titus 2:9

"Exhort servants to be obedient unto their own masters, and to please them well in all things; not answering again;"

If you were to read this verse to the unions that are working today and their leaders, they certainly would not think it was something they should follow today. But it is the position that Christians should take, despite the contradictions of their unions who believe in striking and picketing against their *"masters"* if they don't get their way. It goes against them.

If Christians are in a labor union and disobey this verse, they are wrong. When I taught in the school district of Philadelphia and the teachers' union went out on strike, I continued working in obedience to this verse. I got spit on and rebuked by those who were picketing, but I still kept working because God's Words instructed me to.

> **THE MEANING OF THE GREEK WORD, DOULOS**
> The Greek Word for *"servants"* is DOULOS. Some of the meanings of this Greek Word are:
> > *"1) a slave, bondman, man of servile condition; 1a) a slave; 1b) metaph., one who gives himself up to another's will*

> *those whose service is used by Christ in extending and advancing His cause among men; 1c) devoted to another to the disregard of one's own interests; 2) a servant, attendant."*

That is a very clear meaning of what "*servants*" are to do regarding their "*masters*." Of course, if their masters instruct them to do something contrary to the Words of God, they should not obey such an instruction.

THE MEANING OF THE GREEK WORD, HUPOTASSO

The Greek Word for "*obey*" is HUPOTASSO. Some of the meanings of this Greek Word are:

> "*1) to arrange under, to subordinate; 2) to subject, put in subjection; 3) to subject one's self, obey; 4) to submit to one's control; 5) to yield to one's admonition or advice; 6) to obey, be subject; It is a Greek military term meaning "to arrange [troop divisions] in a miliary fashion under the command of a leader". In non-military use, it was "a voluntary attitude of giving in, cooperating, assuming responsibility, and carrying a burden."*

This is a very clear meaning of what "*obey*" means. There is no ambiguity about it. As I have said before, if something is ordered that would contradict the Words of God, this order should not be obeyed no matter what the result might be.

THE MEANING OF THE GREEK WORD, ANTILEGO

The Greek Word For "*answering again*" is ANTILEGO. Some of the meanings of this Greek word are:

> "*1) to speak against, gainsay, contradict; 2) to oppose one's self to one, decline to obey him, declare one's self against him, refuse to have anything you do with him.*"

Verses On Servants

- **Romans 6:16a**

"Know ye not, that to whom ye yield yourselves servants to obey, his servants ye are to whom ye obey;"

Genuine Christians should be very careful whom they obey and follow. It should not be evil people or evil practices that are contrary to God's Words. They should be servants of God, not servants of evil things.

- **Romans 6:18-19**

"Being then made free from sin, ye became the servants of righteousness. I speak after the manner of men because of the infirmity of your flesh: for as ye have yielded your members servants to uncleanness and to iniquity unto iniquity; even so now yield your members servants to righteousness unto holiness."

AFTER SALVATION--SERVANTS OF RIGHTEOUSNESS

Once true Christians have been saved and redeemed, they become "*servants of righteousness*" and should yield themselves to righteousness and holiness.

- **Romans 6:22**

"But now being made free from sin, and become servants to God, ye have your fruit unto holiness, and the end everlasting life."

True Christians are "*servants to God*" and should act that way in full obedience to God's Words in the Bible.

- **1 Corinthians 7:23**

"Ye are bought with a price; be not ye the servants of men."

The temptation is great to serve people, but genuine Christians must always be servants of God first and foremost.

- **Ephesians 6:5-6**

"Servants, be obedient to them that are *your* masters according to the flesh, with fear and trembling, in singleness of your heart, as unto Christ; Not with eyeservice, as menpleasers; but as the servants of Christ, doing the will of God from the heart;"

Those genuine Christians who are servants in some store or organization should be obedient to their rulers not only when they are watching them. They should serve them just like they would serve the Lord Jesus Christ (provided nothing required would violate the Words of God.

- **Philippians 1:1a**

"Paul and Timotheus, the <u>servants of Jesus Christ</u>,"

Both Paul and Pastor Timothy were servants of the Lord Jesus Christ, ministering to Him and for Him.

- **Colossians 3:22**

"<u>Servants, obey in all things *your* masters</u> according to the flesh; not with eyeservice, as menpleasers; but in singleness of heart, fearing God:"

They should obey their masters in all things except the things that are contrary to God's Words.

- **1 Timothy 6:1**

"Let as many <u>servants as are under the yoke</u> count their own masters worthy of all honour, that the name of God and *his* doctrine be not blasphemed."

CHRISTIANS SHOULD HONOR THEIR EMPLOYERS

True Christians should honor their employers as worthy of all honor in order that God's Name and doctrine will not be blasphemed.

- **1 Peter 2:18**

"<u>Servants, *be* subject to *your* masters</u> with all fear; not only to the good and gentle, but also to the froward."

Other Verses On Masters

- **Matthew 6:24**

"<u>No man can serve two masters</u>: for either he will hate the one, and love the other; or else he will hold to the one, and despise the other. Ye cannot serve God and mammon."

If people have two masters or employers, they can't serve both at the same time. Genuine Christians cannot serve both God and the evil Satanic world.

- **Matthew 23:10**

"Neither be ye called masters: for <u>one is your Master, *even* Christ</u>."

This word for "master" is "teacher." The Lord Jesus Christ is the only Divine and perfect Teacher.

- **Ephesians 6:9**

"And, ye <u>masters</u>, do the same things unto them, <u>forbearing threatening</u>: knowing that <u>your Master also is in heaven</u>; neither is there respect of persons with him."

True Christians with present masters-employers ought to work that way too. They should not threaten their employees or treat them unfairly.
- **Colossians 4:1**
"Masters, give unto *your* servants that which is just and equal; knowing that ye also have a Master in heaven."

CHRISTIAN EMPLOYERS SHOULD BE FAIR AND JUST
Genuine Christian masters or employers should give their servants what is just and equal, taking good care of them.

Titus 2:10
"**Not purloining, but shewing all good fidelity; that they may adorn the doctrine of God our Saviour in all things.**"

THE MEANING OF THE GREEK WORD, NOSPHIZOMAI
The Greek Word for "*purloin*" is NOSPHIZOMAI. Some of the meanings of this Word are:

> "*1) to set apart, separate, divide; 2) to set apart or separate for one's self; 3) to purloin, embezzle, withdraw covertly and appropriate to one's own use.*"

Since that Greek Word is a negative in the Greek present tense, it means to stop an action which is already present. Apparently, some of those servants in Pastor Titus's church were stealing things from someone. Instead, these servants should show all good faithfulness and adorn God's doctrine in all things.

THE MEANING OF THE GREEK WORD, KOSMEO
The Greek Word for "*adorn*" is KOSMEO. Some of the meanings of this Greek Word are:

> "*1) to put in order, arrange, make ready, prepare; 2) to ornament, adore; 3) metaph. to embellish with honour, gain honour.*"

By keeping God's Words and living them out in their daily lives, genuine Christians adorn God's doctrines and teachings.

God the Son is the Saviour of all who have received Him as their Saviour by genuine faith in Him Who died for their sins on the cross.

Titus 2:11

" For the grace of God that bringeth salvation hath appeared to all men,"

THE MEANING OF THE GREEK WORD, CHARIS

The Greek Word for "*grace*" is CHARIS. Some of the meanings of this Greek Word are:

> "*1) grace; 1a) that which affords joy, pleasure, delight, sweetness, charm, loveliness: grace of speech; 2) good will, loving-kindness, favour; 2a) of the merciful kindness by which God, exerting his holy influence upon souls, turns them to Christ, keeps, strengthens, increases them in Christian faith, knowledge, affection, and kindles them to the exercise of the Christian virtues; 3) what is due to grace 3a) the spiritual condition of one governed by the power of divine grace; 3b) the token or proof of grace, benefit; 3b1) a gift of grace; 3b2) benefit, bounty; 4) thanks, (for benefits, services, favours), recompense, reward.*"

This is a Word that has a wideness of meanings. God's grace is a benefit, bounty and gift for which no one in the world has deserved in the past, deserves in the present, or will deserve in the future.

In this verse, God's grace and bounty brings salvation to those and for those who fulfilled His method of receiving it. It is for those who:

(1) Realize they are lost sinners;

(2) Realize that the Lord Jesus Christ died for their sins on the cross; and

(3) Places their sincere faith and trust in the Lord Jesus Christ as their Saviour. This salvation that God provided "*appeared to all men.*"

THE MEANING OF THE GREEK WORD, EPIPHAINO

The Greek Word for "*appeared*" is EPIPHAINO. Some of the meanings of this Greek Word are:

> "*1) to show to or upon; 1a) to bring to*

> *light; 2) to appear, become visible; 2a) of stars; 3) to become clearly known, to show one's self."*

This verse teaches that God's grace that brings salvation appeared to all men (not only to some "elect" group as the hyper-Calvinists teach). That does not mean that all men and women are genuine Christians and will all go to Heaven. That so-called universalism is a heresy. What it does mean is that His salvation and way to obtain it has been made visible and clearly known by the teachings of the New Testament that were written and spread abroad from the first century and onward.

Verses On Grace

- **Luke 2:40b**

". . . and the grace of God was upon him."

God's grace was upon the Lord Jesus Christ. Everybody could see God's grace upon our Saviour while He was on this earth.

- **Acts 15:40**

"And Paul chose Silas, and departed, being recommended by the brethren unto the grace of God."

Paul and Silas were recommended by the Christian brethren unto God's grace.

- **Acts 20:24**

"But none of these things move me, neither count I my life dear unto myself, so that I might finish my course with joy, and the ministry, which I have received of the Lord Jesus, to testify the gospel of the grace of God."

PAUL WAS FAITHFUL TO CHRIST'S COMMISSION

Paul was moved by those who told him not to go to Jerusalem because they would put him in prison and/or kill him. Paul wanted to testify ab out the gospel of God's grace and this he did. He preached the gospel to those in prison, to the prisoners in the ship bound for Rome, and to those on the desert island where he was shipwrecked. He was faithful in this mission for the Lord Jesus Christ.

- **Romans 5:15**

"But not as the offence, so also *is* the free gift. For if through the offence of one many be dead, much more <u>the grace of God</u>, and <u>the gift by grace</u>, *which is* by one man, Jesus Christ, <u>hath abounded unto many</u>."

God's grace and the gospel of his grace has abounded for all the thousands of years past and will continue to abound for all the years in the future.

- **1 Corinthians 1:4**

"I thank my God always on your behalf, <u>for the grace of God which is given you by Jesus Christ</u>;"

God's grace was given to those in Corinth through the Lord Jesus Christ.

- **1 Corinthians 15:10**

"But <u>by the grace of God I am what I am</u>: and <u>his grace</u> which *was bestowed* upon me <u>was not in vain</u>; but I laboured more abundantly than they all: yet not I, but <u>the grace of God which was with me</u>."

Just as the Apostle Paul was then, genuine Christians today are what they are by the grace of God. If you are a true Christian, has God's grace and salvation been given to you in vain? Are you laboring, by God's grace, for the Lord Jesus Christ each day? If not, why not?

- **2 Corinthians 6:1**

"We then, *as* workers together *with him*, beseech *you* also <u>that ye receive not the grace of God in vain</u>."

Paul did not want the genuine Christians at Corinth to have received God's grace in vain and to no purpose. He wanted them to serve their Saviour! This is what all true Christians should do!

- **Galatians 2:21**

"<u>I do not frustrate the grace of God</u>: for if righteousness *come* by the law, then Christ is dead in vain."

RIGHTEOUSNESS CAN'T COME BY MOSES' LAW

Righteousness with God can never come through the Law of Moses. It comes to genuine Christians by true faith in the Lord Jesus Christ's death on Calvary for their sins. True Christians today are not under any of the three divisions of the Law of Moses. They are under God's grace in this present time.

- **Ephesians 3:2**
"If ye have heard of <u>the dispensation of the grace of God</u> which is given me to you-ward:"

Right now, genuine Christians are in that "*dispensation of the grace of God*" rather than any part of the Mosaic Law.

- **Ephesians 3:7**
"Whereof I was made a minister, according to <u>the gift of the grace of God given unto me</u> by the effectual working of his power."

Paul was made a minister of the gospel of the Lord Jesus Christ in accord with God's gift and power.

- **Hebrews 2:9**
"But we see Jesus, who was made a little lower than the angels for the suffering of death, crowned with glory and honour; that <u>he by the grace of God should taste death for every man</u>."

This was God's **provision** for every man, woman, and child. But they must act on this provision by genuine faith in the Lord Jesus Christ before that provision is able to take affect in their lives.

This truth is contrary to the heresy of the gospel of the hyper-Calvinists. They deny Christ's provision of salvation for every person. They say that the Lord Jesus Christ tasted death, not for every person, but only for a small group of people they call "the elect." They falsely teach that all of the "non-elect" ones are lost eternally and are destined for the Lake of Fire in Hell.

Titus 2:12

"Teaching us that, denying ungodliness and worldly lusts, we should live soberly, righteously, and godly, in this present world;"

The grace of God teaches the genuine Christians many things. The grace of God is a teaching ministry. There are five things that Paul mentioned to Titus that the grace of God teaches them.

1. **God's Grace Teaches Us To Deny Ungodliness.**

THE MEANING OF THE GREEK WORD, PAIDEUO

The Greek Word for *"deny"* is PAIDEUO. Some of the meanings of that Greek Word are:

"1) to train children; 1a) to be instructed or taught or learn; 1b) to cause one to learn; 2) to chastise;

> *2a) to chastise or castigate with words, to correct; 2a1) of those who are moulding the character of others by reproof and admonition; 2b) of God; 2b1) to chasten by the affliction of evils and calamities; 2c) to chastise with blows, to scourge; 2c1) of a father punishing his son; 2c2) of a judge ordering one to be scourged"*

You'll notice in this definition of *"teach"* that there are many senses of this Greek Word. *"To be instructed or taught"* is probably the closest meaning in these present verses in Titus.

THE MEANING OF THE GREEK WORD, AMEOMAI

The Greek Word for *"deny"* is AMEOMAI. Some of the meanings of this Greek Word are:

> *"1) to deny; 2) to deny someone; 2a) to deny one's self; 2a1) to disregard his own interests or to prove false to himself; 2a2) act entirely unlike himself; 3) to deny, abnegate, abjure; 4) not to accept, to reject, to refuse something offered."*

God's grace teaches genuine Christians to deny any ungodliness whether in thoughts, deeds, associations, companionship, or practices. When faced with ungodliness of any kind, they must just say *"no"* to it.

Verses On Ungodliness

- **Romans 1:18**

"For the wrath of God is revealed from heaven against all ungodliness and unrighteousness of men, who hold the truth in unrighteousness;"

GOD HATES UNGODLINESS AND JUDGES IT

God hates ungodliness and has revealed it many times in the world's history. Look what He did in the universal flood of the earth in Noah's day! Look what He did in the destruction of Sodom and Gomorrah! In these, and other, instances God showed that He was totally against ungodliness. He has prepared the fires of everlasting Hell for those who reject His Son in an ungodly manner of unbelief.

- **Romans 11:26**

"And so all Israel shall be saved: as it is written, There shall come out of Sion the Deliverer, and shall turn away ungodliness from Jacob:"

The Lord Jesus Christ will deliver ungodliness from the Jews when He returns in the second phase of His second coming during His millennial reign.

- **2 Timothy 2:16**

"But shun profane *and* vain babblings: for they will increase unto more ungodliness."

Profanity and empty words will make more ungodliness than being silent and saying nothing.

2. **God's Grace Teaches Us To Deny Worldly Lusts.**

THE MEANING OF THE GREEK WORD, EPITHUMIA

The Greek Word for *"lust"* is EPITHUMIA. Some of the meanings of this Greek Word are:

"1) desire, craving, longing, desire for what is forbidden, lust."

There are many worldly lusts that should be denied including fornication, adultery, homosexuality, lesbianism, incest, lying, stealing, and many, many more.

Verses On Lusts

John 8:44

"Ye are of *your* father the devil, and the lusts of your father ye will do. He was a murderer from the beginning, and abode not in the truth, because there is no truth in him. When he speaketh a lie, he speaketh of his own: for he is a liar, and the father of it."

The Lord Jesus Christ spoke very clearly to the unbelieving and evil Pharisees. He said that they were doing the lusts of their spiritual father–the Devil.

- **Romans 6:12**

"Let not sin therefore reign in your mortal body, that ye should obey it in the lusts thereof."

Paul is speaking to the genuine Christians in Rome that they should stop letting their sin nature reign in their bodies to obey it in its lusts.

- **Romans 13:14**

"But put ye on the Lord Jesus Christ, and make not provision for the flesh, to *fulfil* the lusts *thereof*."

These true Christians in Rome should stop making provision for their flesh to fulfill its many and varied lusts.
- **2 Timothy 2:22**
"Flee also youthful lusts: but follow righteousness, faith, charity, peace, with them that call on the Lord out of a pure heart."

YOUTHFUL LUSTS ARE NOT LIMITED TO YOUTH
Does that mean youthful lusts are only possible for youth? No. youthful lusts can be practiced by genuine Christians, whether they are young or old. They should flee all such lusts.

- **James 4:1**
"From whence come wars and fightings among you? come they not hence, even of your lusts that war in your members?"

The source of wars and fightings is from peoples' lust in members of their bodies.
- **1 Peter 2:11**
"Dearly beloved, I beseech you as strangers and pilgrims, abstain from fleshly lusts, which war against the soul;"

Peter was addressing genuine Christians who were former Jews. He told them to abstain for all the lusts of their flesh that war against their souls.
- **1 Peter 4:3**
"For the time past of our life may suffice us to have wrought the will of the Gentiles, when we walked in lasciviousness, lusts, excess of wine, revellings, banquetings, and abominable idolatries:"

Though in the times past, these true Christians should not continue in such lasciviousness and lusts. The past life should be avoided now that they are new creatures in the Lord Jesus Christ.

3. **God's Grace Teaches Us To Live Soberly.**

THE MEANING OF THE GREEK WORD, SOPHRONOS
The Greek Word for *"soberly"* is SOPHRONOS. Some of the meanings of this Word are:
"1) with sound mind, soberly, temperately, discreetly."

Genuine Christians are taught by God's grace to live with a sound mind, temperately, and discretely. soberly. They should be in control of themselves at all times.

4. **God's Grace Teaches Us To Live Righteously.**

True Christians should live according to the righteousness of the Scriptures. The Words of God found in the Bible are the only place they can find what God means by "*righteousness.*" They must not go by the standards of the world, but by God's standards alone.

5. **God's Grace Teaches Us To Live Godly.**

God's grace teaches genuine Christians to live their lives in a godly manner. This is getting more difficult as the years roll by and ungodliness increases immensely. Far too many people live ungodly lives. They use God's Name in vain by swearing. Radio, television, Hollywood movies, books, and the Internet are loaded with ungodliness. Only by being controlled by God the Holy Spirit Who lives within them can true Christians live godly lives in the midst of an ungodly, worldly, and Satanically led world.

An Important Verse On Godly

- 2 Timothy 3:12

"Yea, and all that will live godly in Christ Jesus shall suffer persecution."

WILLING TO BE GODLY BRINGS PERSECUTION

Paul told Pastor Timothy that all genuine Christians who are willing to live godly in the Lord Jesus Christ shall suffer persecution. This is not just an opinion, but it is a fact.

Titus 2:13

"**Looking for that blessed hope, and the glorious appearing of the great God and our Saviour Jesus Christ;**"

MEANING OF THE GREEK WORD, PROSDECHOMAI

The Greek Word for "*looking*" is PROSDECHOMAI. Some of the meanings of this Greek Word are:

> "*1) to receive to one's self, to admit, to give access to one's self; 1a) to admit one, receive one into intercourse and companionship; 1b) to receive one (coming from some place); 1c) to accept (not to reject) a thing offered; 2) to expect.*"

Those genuine Christians who abide by all five of the teachings of God's grace (referred in verse 12) should also be looking for and expecting both the blessed hope (the rapture of true Christians) and the glorious appearing (the beginning of the millennial reign) of the Lord Jesus Christ.

The "*blessed hope*" refers to the rapture of all true Christians. Both those who have died and those who are still living will meet the Lord Jesus Christ in the air. Those Christians who have died will have their corruptible bodies transformed to incorruptible bodies. Those true Christians who are still living, will have their mortal bodies transformed into immortal bodies (1 Corinthians 15:49-54).

RAPTURE POSITIONS–FIVE FALSE AND ONE TRUE

The rapture has at least five false teachings concerning it and only one true and Biblical teaching.

(1) It is not only a partial rapture of just some of the genuine Christians. (Partial Rapture Error)
(2) It does not take place in the middle of the Tribulation's seven years. (Mid-Tribulation Rapture error)
(3) It does not take place at the end of the Tribulation's seven years. (Post-Tribulation Rapture error)
(4) It does not take place in the pre-wrath section of the Tribulation's seven years. (Pre-Wrath Rapture error)
(5) It is not eliminated altogether.
(6) It <u>DOES</u> take place before any part of the Tribulation's seven years. (Pre-Tribulation Rapture truth)

"*The glorious appearing*" of the Lord Jesus Christ will take place after the seven year Tribulation Period. The Lord Jesus Christ will come down from Heaven and set His feet on the Mount of Olives where He ascended to Heaven after His bodily resurrection. He will then set up His millennial kingdom of 1,000-year reign upon the earth.

Verses On Looking

- **Mark 10:27**

"And <u>Jesus looking upon them</u> saith, With men *it is* impossible, but not with God: for with God all things are possible."

The Lord Jesus Christ looked on those unbelieving Pharisees in an effort to straighten them on their many errors.
- **Luke 6:10**
"And looking round about upon them all, he said unto the man, Stretch forth thy hand. And he did so: and his hand was restored whole as the other. "

As the Lord Jesus Christ healed this man, He looked around at every one who was present at that time.
- **Luke 9:62**
"And Jesus said unto him, No man, having put his hand to the plough, and looking back, is fit for the kingdom of God."

Once people have truly trusted in the Lord Jesus Christ as their Saviour, they should not look back on their past lives and wish to return to their old lives and ways. They should continue serving their Saviour.
- **Hebrews 12:2**
"Looking unto Jesus the author and finisher of *our* faith; who for the joy that was set before him endured the cross, despising the shame, and is set down at the right hand of the throne of God."

> **CHRISTIANS SHOULD LOOK TO THE SAVIOUR**
>
> True Christians should look unto their Lord Jesus Christ for all of their needs and for His strength for them to continue to serve Him.

- **Luke 21:26**
"Men's hearts failing them for fear, and for looking after those things which are coming on the earth: for the powers of heaven shall be shaken."

People will be fearful when God shakes the heavens as never before seen.
- **Matthew 14:19**
"And he commanded the multitude to sit down on the grass, and took the five loaves, and the two fishes, and looking up to heaven, he blessed, and brake, and gave the loaves to *his* disciples, and the disciples to the multitude."

At the feeding of the five thousand, the Lord Jesus Christ looked up to Heaven as He broke the five loaves of bread and gave them to His disciples to distribute to the people.

- **Hebrews 12:2**
"Looking unto Jesus the author and finisher of *our* faith; who for the joy that was set before him endured the cross, despising the shame, and is set down at the right hand of the throne of God." Genuine Christians should be looking unto the Lord Jesus Christ for help, assistance, strength, and guidance as they live their lives in this corrupt and wicked world around them.

Titus 2:14

"Who gave himself for us, that he might redeem us from all iniquity, and purify unto himself a peculiar people zealous of good works."

The Lord Jesus Christ "*gave Himself for us.*" That took place on the cross at Calvary.

THE MEANING OF THE GREEK WORD, DIDOMI

The Greek Word for "*gave*" is DIDOMI. Some of the meanings of this Greek Word are:

> "1) to give; 2) to give something to someone; 2a) of one's own accord to give one something, to his advantage; 2a1) to bestow a gift; 2b) to grant, give to one asking, let have; 2c) to supply, furnish, necessary things; 2d) to give over, deliver; 2d1) to reach out, extend, present; 2d2) of a writing; 2d3) to give over to one's care, intrust, commit; 2d3a) something to be administered; 2d3b) to give or commit to some one something to be religiously observed; 2e) to give what is due or obligatory, to pay: wages or reward; 2f) to furnish, endue; 3) to give; 3a) to cause, profuse, give forth from one's self 3a1) to give, hand out lots; 3b) to appoint to an office; 3c) to cause to come forth, i.e. as the sea, death and Hell are said to give up the dead who have been engulfed or received by them; 3c) to give one to someone as his own 3c1) as an

> *object of his saving care; 3c2) to give one to someone, to follow him as a leader and master; 3c3) to give one to someone to care for his interests; 3c4) to give one to someone to whom he already belonged, to return; 4) to grant or permit one; 4a) to commission."*

While it is true that the Lord Jesus Christ gave Himself on the cross of Calvary, in the hyper-Calvinist churches around the world today, there is much heresy being taught about the purpose of that death. In the phrase, *"gave Himself for us,"* let me take this up in two parts.

1. **The Meaning Of "For."**

THE MEANING OF THE GREEK WORD, HUPER

The Greek Word translated *"for"* is HUPER. Some of the meanings of this Greek Word are:

"1) in behalf of, for the sake of; 2) over, beyond, more than; 3) more, beyond, over."

It is clear that the Lord Jesus Christ gave Himself on the cross in behalf of, and for the sake of the *"us"* in this verse.

2. **The Meaning Of "Us."**

Contrary to the heresy of the hyper-Calvinists who erroneously teach that the Lord Jesus Christ gave Himself and died only for a small group of *"elect"* people, I believe this *"us"* refers to every human being who ever lived. I believe the Bible teaches clearly that the Lord Jesus Christ made provision and died for the sins of every person who ever lived. John 3:16-18 and many, many other verses make this clear:

> *"For God so loved **the world**, that he gave his only begotten Son that **whosoever believeth in him** should not perish, but have everlasting life. For God sent not his son into the world to condemn the world; but **that the world through him might be saved. He that believeth on him is not condemned; but he that believeth not is condemned** already, because he hath not believed in the name of the only begotten Son of God."* (John 3:16-18)

To those who genuinely trust the Lord Jesus Christ as their Saviour, He redeems from all sin and iniquity. After their salvation, He wants to purify these true Christians as a peculiar people who are zealous in doing good works for their Saviour.

THE MEANING OF THE GREEK WORD, PERIOUSIOS

The Greek Word for *"peculiar"* is PERIOUSIOS. Some of the meanings of this Greek Word are:

"1) that which is one's own, belonging to one's possessions; 1a) a people selected by God from the other nations for his own possession."

THE MEANING OF THE GREEK WORD, ZELOTES

The Greek Word for *"zealous"* is ZELOTES. Some of the meanings of this Geek Word are:

"1) one burning with zeal, a zealot; 2) used of God as jealous of any rival and sternly vindicating."

Another Verse On Christ Dying For The Sins Of Every Person Who Ever Lived.

- 1 Timothy 2:6

"Who gave himself a ransom for all, to be testified in due time." The ransom paid by the Lord Jesus Christ was not for the elect only. That position is a heresy that is taught by hyper-Calvinists all around the world. No! He gave Himself a ransom for all! That includes every person who ever was born and lived on this earth. He was and is their Substitute in Whom they must truly trust and believe in order for them to be genuine Christians.

Verses On Redemption

- 1 Corinthians 1:30

"But of him are ye in Christ Jesus, who of God is made unto us wisdom, and righteousness, and sanctification, and redemption: For the genuine Christians, the Lord Jesus Christ is made their redemption.

- **Ephesians 1:7**

"In whom we have redemption through his blood, the forgiveness of sins, according to the riches of his grace;"

True Christians have redemption by means of true faith in the Lord Jesus Christ and His shed blood.
- **Hebrews 9:12**
"Neither by the blood of goats and calves, but by his own blood he entered in once into the holy place, having obtained eternal redemption for us."

Genuine Christians have obtained eternal redemption by the finished work of the Lord Jesus Christ.
- **Galatians 4:4**
"But when the fulness of the time was come, God sent forth his Son, made of a woman, made under the law, To redeem them that were under the law, that we might receive the adoption of sons."

God the Father sent God the Son to redeem those who put their genuine faith and trust in the Lord Jesus Christ.

Verses On Good Works
- **Ephesians 2:10**
"For we are his workmanship, created in Christ Jesus unto good works, which God hath before ordained that we should walk in them."

Good works will not save anyone. But after true Christians have been redeemed, God expects them to do good works for Him.
- **1 Timothy 6:18**
"That they do good, that they be rich in good works, ready to distribute, willing to communicate;"

Genuine Christians should be rich in "good works" for the Lord Jesus Christ after their salvation.
- **Titus 2:7**
"In all things shewing thyself a pattern of good works: in doctrine shewing uncorruptness, gravity, sincerity,"

Pastor Titus was to show himself as a pattern of good works to exemplify and teach others in his congregation at Ephesus.
- **Titus 3:8**
"This is a faithful saying, and these things I will that thou affirm constantly, that they which have believed in God might be careful to maintain good works. These things are good and profitable unto men."

God wants all true Christians to continue to maintain good works. They are good and profitable to those who see them.

- **Titus 3:14**

"And let ours also <u>learn to maintain good works</u> for necessary uses, that they be not unfruitful."

Again, Pastor Titus emphasized that his congregation should maintain good works which are needed for others to behold.

- **Matthew 5:16**

"Let your light so shine before men, <u>that they may see your good works, and glorify your Father</u> which is in heaven."

The Lord Jesus Christ told His disciples to maintain good works which would glorify their Father which is in Heaven.

Titus 2:15

"These things speak and exhort and rebuke with all authority. Let no man despise thee."

All three of these Greek verbs in this verse are in the Greek present tense. This indicates a continuous action in all three of the verbs. Paul told Pastor Titus that he must continue to do three things: (1) continue to speak; (2) continue to exhort, and (3) continue to rebuke with all authority.

THE MEANING OF THE GREEK WORD, PARAKALEO

The Greek Word for "*exhort*" is PARAKALEO. Some of the meanings of this Greek Word are:

"1) to call to one's side, call for, summon; 2) to address, speak to, (call to, call upon), which may be done in the way of exhortation, entreaty, comfort, instruction, etc.; 2a) to admonish, exhort; 2b) to beg, entreat, beseech; 2b1) to strive to appease by entreaty; 2c) to console, to encourage and strengthen by consolation, to comfort; 2c1) to receive consolation, be comforted; 2d) to encourage, strengthen; 2e) exhorting and comforting and encouraging; 2f) to instruct, teach"

THE MEANING OF THE GREEK WORD, ELEGCHO

The Greek Word for *"rebuke"* is ELEGCHO. Some of the meanings of this Greek Word are:

"1) to convict, refute, confute; 1a) generally with a suggestion of shame of the person convicted; 1b) by conviction to bring to the light, to expose; 2) to find fault with, correct; 2a) by word; 2a1) to reprehend severely, chide, admonish, reprove; 2a2) to call to account, show one his fault, demand an explanation; 2b) by deed; 2b1) to chasten, to punish."

In addition to these three things Titus was to do, there is another order given by Paul. It is a Greek negative command in the Greek present tense. This means to stop an action that is already going on. He was to stop letting people despise him.

THE MEANING OF THE GREEK WORD, PERIPHONEO

The Greek Word for *"despise"* is PERIPHONEO. Some of the meanings of this Greek Word are:

"1) to consider or examine on all sides i.e. carefully, thoroughly; 2) to set one's self in thought beyond (exalt one's self in thought above) a person or a thing; 3) to contemn, to despise."

As in Pastor Titus' case, so pastors today–in their preaching and teaching as well as at other times–should do their best to take heed to these actions which should be accomplished *"with all authority."*

Verses On Rebuke

- **Proverbs 9:8**

"Reprove not a scorner, lest he hate thee: rebuke a wise man, and he will love thee."

There must be a wise use of rebuke. Wise men will receive it well, but not scorners.

- **Luke 17:3**

"Take heed to yourselves: If thy brother trespass against thee, rebuke him; and if he repent, forgive him."

Rebuke and forgiveness both have a place when dealing with family members in the physical family, in the spiritual family.

- **1 Timothy 5:20**
  "Them that sin rebuke before all, that others also may fear."

Paul is instructing Pastor Titus how to deal with other elders or pastors who sin. Before a pastor is to be rebuked, the charges against him should be made by at least two or three witnesses. Then, and only then, should he be rebuked before all. This implies that the sin should be made public. Too often, pastoral sins are kept covered up which is against God's commands.

- **2 Timothy 4:2**
  "Preach the word; be instant in season, out of season; reprove, rebuke, exhort with all longsuffering and doctrine."

Rebuking, along with reproving and exhorting were Pastor Titus's orders from the Apostle Paul. All of these actions, however, should be accomplished with both longsuffering and doctrine.

- **Titus 1:13**
  "This witness is true. Wherefore rebuke them sharply, that they may be sound in the faith;"

The Cretans were *"liars, evil beasts, slow bellies."* Because of these evil conditions, Pastor Titus should rebuke them sharply so that they might be sound in the doctrines of the Bible. Pastors today should follow this example and continue to rebuke any and all kinds of false doctrines or actions.

- **Revelation 3:19**
  "As many as I love, I rebuke and chasten: be zealous therefore, and repent."

The Lord Jesus Christ teaches in this verse that part of a person's genuine love for other people involves proper rebuke when it is needed, even if it is not well received.

Verses On Authority

- **Matthew 7:28-29**
  "And it came to pass, when Jesus had ended these sayings, the people were astonished at his doctrine: For he taught them as one having authority, and not as the scribes."

The Lord Jesus Christ taught His doctrine with all authority, not as the scribes taught.

- **2 Corinthians 10:8**
  "For though I should boast somewhat more of our authority, which the Lord hath given us for edification, and not for your destruction, I should not be ashamed:

Even if Paul should boast of his authority as an apostle, he was not ashamed when he gave them proper edification from the Bible's truth. He didn't want to destroy them.
- **1 Timothy 2:12**
"But <u>I suffer not a woman to teach, nor to usurp authority over the man</u>, but to be in silence."

This is one of the many verses against women preachers who are preaching by the thousands in all different denominations, including Baptists, Lutherans, Episcopalians, Presbyterians, and many more denominations. That is a bad use of authority.

Titus Chapter Three

Titus 3:1

"Put them in mind to be subject to principalities and powers, to obey magistrates, to be ready to every good work,"

In the first two verses of this Chapter 3, the Apostle Paul asks Pastor Titus to remind his congregation about six important things.

1. <u>Pastor Titus Was To Remind His Church To Be Subject To Principalities And Powers.</u>

> **THE MEANING OF THE GREEK WORD, HUPOTASSO**
>
> The Greek Word for *"be subject"* is HUPOTASSO. It is in the Greek present tense which indicates a continuous action. This subjection should be continual (unless, of course, there would be some things that are contrary to the Biblical teachings.) Some of the meanings of this Greek Word are:
>
>> *"1) to arrange under, to subordinate; 2) to subject, put in subjection; 3) to subject one's self, obey; 4) <u>to submit to one's control</u>; 5) to yield to one's admonition or advice; 6) to obey, be subject; It was also a Greek military term meaning "to arrange [troop divisions] in a miliary fashion under the command of a leader". In non-military use, it was "a voluntary attitude of giving in, cooperating, assuming responsibility, and carrying a burden."*

This continuous subjection or obedience is to be given (unless contrary to the clear teachings of the Bible, as mentioned above) to two entities: (1) principalities; and (2) powers.

THE MEANING OF THE GREEK WORD, ARCHE

The Greek Word for *"principalities"* is ARCHE. As you will notice, it has a wide range of meanings. Some of the meanings of this Greek Word are:

"1) beginning, origin; 2) the person or thing that commences, the first person or thing in a series, <u>the leader</u>; 3) that by which anything begins to be, the origin, the active cause; 4) the extremity of a thing 4a) of the corners of a sail; 5) the first place, principality, <u>rule, magistracy</u>; 5a) of angels and demons."

THE MEANING OF THE GREEK WORD, EXOUSIA

The Greek Word for *"powers"* is EXOUSIA. Some of the many meanings of this Greek Word are:

"1) power of choice, liberty of doing as one pleases; 1a) leave or permission; 2) physical and mental power; 2a) the ability or strength with which one is endued, which he either possesses or exercises; 3) the power of authority (influence) and of right (privilege); 4) the power of rule or government (the power of him whose will and commands must be submitted to by others and obeyed); 1) power of choice, liberty of doing as one pleases; 1a) leave or permission; 2) physical and mental power; 2a) the ability or strength with which one is endued, which he either possesses or exercises; 3) the power of authority (influence) and of right (privilege); 4) <u>the power of rule or government (the power of him whose will and commands must be submitted to by others and obeyed)</u>; 4a)

> *universally; 4a1) authority over mankind; 4b) specifically; 4b1) the power of judicial decisions; 4b2) of authority to manage domestic affairs; 4c) metonymically; 4c1) a thing subject to authority or rule; 4c1a) jurisdiction; 4c2) one who possesses authority; 4c2a) a ruler, a human magistrate; 4c2b) the leading and more powerful among created beings superior to man, spiritual potentates; 4d) a sign of the husband's authority over his wife; 4d1) the veil with which propriety required a women to cover herself; 4e) the sign of regal authority, a crown."*

Since there are so many definitions of these three previous words, I have <u>underlined</u> the meanings that seem to be the closest for the understanding of this verse.

2. Pastor Titus Was To Remind His Church To Obey Magistrates.

> **THE MEANING OF THE GREEK WORD, PEITHARCHEO**
> The Greek Word for *"obey magistrates"* is PEITHARCHEO. This verb is also in the Greek present tense and means obedience is to be continuous [unless, of course, it is in violation to the Bible's teachings.] One of the meanings of this Greek Word is:
> *"1) to obey (a ruler or a superior)."*

This Greek Word seems to be more general in its meaning and application. It seems to imply obedience either to a "ruler" or any one who is "superior" in office or power to the genuine Christians in Titus' church. As mentioned above, this obedience should only be followed if the things commanded are not contrary to the Bible's teachings.

Verses On Not Obeying If Laws Contradict The Bible

Those ministers who have been selected to round up people to put them in the FEMA prison camps have been told to use Romans 13:1-4 to insist that people obey these ministers and leave their homes. Notice what kind of *"rulers"* are referred to in these verses. They are ONLY those who are a terror to evil works and not to good

works. Genuine Christians have no need to obey the orders of evil and not Biblically good rulers. The following verses define very clearly what Biblical government is.
- **Romans 13:1-4**
  "Let every soul be subject unto the higher powers. For there is no power but of God: the powers that be are ordained of God. Whosoever therefore resisteth the power, resisteth the ordinance of God: and they that resist shall receive to themselves damnation. For **rulers are not a terror to good works, but to the evil**. *Wilt thou then not be afraid of the power?* **do that which is good, and thou shalt have praise of the same**: *For he is the minister of God to thee for good. But if thou do that which is evil, be afraid; for he beareth not the sword in vain: for* **he is the minister of God, a revenger to execute wrath upon him that doeth evil**.*"*

Obey the authorities but, in doing so, never disobey the Words of God.

The Apostles Disobeyed Roman Orders
- **Acts 5:29**

"Then Peter and the *other* apostles answered and said, We ought to obey God rather than men."

This is an illustration of the apostles' disobedience of Roman law because of its being contrary to God's command to preach and teach the gospel.
- **Acts 5:40**

"And to him they agreed: and when they had called the apostles, and beaten *them*, they commanded that they should not speak in the name of Jesus, and let them go. And they departed from the presence of the council, rejoicing that they were counted worthy to suffer shame for his name. And daily in the temple, and in every house, they ceased not to teach and preach Jesus Christ."

THE APOSTLES OBEYED GOD RATHER THAN MAN

The apostles obeyed God rather than men and continued to preach the Lord Jesus Christ. That is a good example that should be followed by true Christians today.

3. **Pastor Titus Was To Remind His Church To Be Ready To Every Good Work.**

> **THE MEANING OF THE GREEK WORD, HETOIMOS**
> The Greek Word for *"ready"* is HETOIMOS. The verb "to be" is in the Greek present tense which calls for a continuous and uninterrupted readiness. Some of the meanings of this Greek Word are:
>> *"1) prepare ready; 1a) of things; 1a1) ready at hand; 1a2) opportune, seasonable; 1b) of persons; 1b1) <u>ready, prepared</u>; 1b1a) to do something; 1b1b) to receive one coming."*

This would imply that every true Christian in Pastor Titus' church (and true Christians today) should be continually and always ready and prepared to do Biblically good works. They should never be off duty in this area. These good works are the fruit of their being redeemed and saved by genuine faith in the Lord Jesus Christ.

Titus 3:2

"To speak evil of no man, to be no brawlers, but gentle, shewing all meekness unto all men."

4. **Pastor Titus Was To Remind His Church To Speak Evil Of No Man.**

> **THE MEANING OF THE GREEK WORD, BLASPHEMEO**
> The Greek Word for *"speak evil"* is BLASPHEMEO. Some of the meanings of this Greek Word are:
>> *"1) to speak reproachfully, rail at, revile, calumniate, blaspheme; 2) to be evil spoken of, reviled, railed at."*

This verb is in the Greek present tense which signifies a continuous action. It would certainly include not speaking lies or falsehoods about anyone. It would include not criticizing in an abusive or in an angrily and insulting manner.

5. **Pastor Titus Was To Remind His Church Not To Be Brawlers.**

> **THE MEANING OF THE GREEK WORD, AMACHOS**
> The Greek Word for "*brawlers*" is AMACHOS. Some of the meanings of this Greek Word are:
> "*1) not to be withstood, invincible; 2) not contentious; 3) abstaining from fighting.*"

The Greek for "*be*" is in the Greek present tense. The meaning is that the genuine Christians are continuously not to be brawlers. They should never engage in fist-fighting except in their own, their family's, or their friends' self-defense.

6. **Pastor Titus Was To Remind His Church To Be Gentle.**

> **THE MEANING OF THE GREEK WORD, EPIEIKES**
> The Greek Word for "*gentle*" is EPIEIKES. Some of the meanings of this Greek Word are:
> "*1) seemingly, suitable; 2) equitable, fair, mild, gentle.*"

This trait should characterize all true Christians in Pastor Titus' day as well in our present days.

7. **Pastor Titus Was To Remind His Church To Show Meekness To All People.**

> **THE MEANING OF THE GREEK WORD, PRAOTES**
> The Greek Word for "*meekness*" is PRAOTES. Some of the meanings for this Greek Word are:
> "*1) gentleness, mildness, meekness*"

This is to be a gentleness and mildness in the genuine Christians' manner and character. There is no thought of weakness in this Greek Word. This does not preclude Christians to have the strength to stand up strongly against all evil that God's Word is against.

Verses On Speaking Evil

- **1 Peter 3:16**

"Having a good conscience; that, whereas they speak evil of you, as of evildoers, they may be ashamed that falsely accuse your good conversation in Christ."

Titus Expounded Verse by Verse

Regardless of how many people speak evil of genuine Christians, the Christians should have a good conscience about it and hope that the accusers might be ashamed.

- **Jude 1:10**

"But these speak evil of those things which they know not: but what they know naturally, as brute beasts, in those things they corrupt themselves."

Many people today also speak evil of things they don't know anything about. This is foolish, but it still is done often.

Verses On Gentle

- **2 Timothy 2:24**

"And the servant of the Lord must not strive; but be gentle unto all *men*, apt to teach, patient,"

> **FIRM IN DEFENDING GOD'S WORDS, BUT GENTLE**
>
> This doesn't mean genuine Christians can't be firm and strong in defense of the Words of God, but they are to be gentle to all.

- **James 3:17**

"But the wisdom that is from above is first pure, then peaceable, gentle, *and* easy to be intreated, full of mercy and good fruits, without partiality, and without hypocrisy."

Wisdom from God, given in His Words, is gentle wisdom.

Verses On Meekness

- **2 Corinthians 10:1**

"Now I Paul myself beseech you by the meekness and gentleness of Christ, who in presence *am* base among you, but being absent am bold toward you:"

The Lord Jesus Christ is the example of meekness for all genuine Christians.

- **Galatians 5:23**

"Meekness, temperance: against such there is no law."

One of the fruits when true Christians are controlled by God the Holy Spirit is manifested in meekness.

- **Ephesians 4:1**

"I therefore, the prisoner of the Lord, beseech you that ye walk worthy of the vocation wherewith ye are called, With all lowliness and meekness, with longsuffering, forbearing one another in love;"

Paul was a prisoner in a Roman prison at the time. He urged the genuine Christians in Ephesus to walk with all meekness in their lives. This should be true of such Christians today.

- **Colossians 3:12**

"<u>Put on</u> therefore, as the elect of God, holy and beloved, bowels of mercies, kindness, humbleness of mind, <u>meekness</u>, longsuffering;"

This means that the true Christians at Colosse were to put on meekness just as they were to put on some article of clothing.

- **1 Timothy 6:11**

"But thou, <u>O man of God</u>, flee these things; and <u>follow after</u> righteousness, godliness, faith, love, patience, <u>meekness</u>."

Pastor Timothy was told by the Apostle Paul to flee various sins, but follow after meekness and other Godly things.

- **2 Timothy 2:25**

"<u>In meekness instructing those that oppose themselves</u>; if God peradventure will give them repentance to the acknowledging of the truth;"

Pastor Timothy was to instruct with meekness those who are in need of salvation.

- **James 1:21**

"Wherefore lay apart all filthiness and superfluity of naughtiness, and <u>receive with meekness the engrafted word</u>, which is able to save your souls."

The Words of God must be received with meekness by true Christians, even if they condemn what they might be thinking, saying, or doing.

- **1 Peter 3:15**

"But sanctify the Lord God in your hearts: and *be* ready always to *give* <u>an answer to every man that asketh you</u> a reason of the hope that is in you <u>with meekness</u> and fear:"

ANSWER QUESTIONS WITH MEEKNESS

In giving their testimony and in answering questions posed by non-Christians, genuine Christians must do this with meekness.

Titus 3:3

"For we ourselves also were sometimes foolish, disobedient, deceived, serving divers lusts and pleasures, living in malice and envy, hateful, and hating one another."

The Apostle Paul describes for Pastor Titus their past life before they became genuine Christians. The Greek Word for "*were*" is in the Greek imperfect tense. This indicates that all these conditions were in their past lives continually. These same things are possible for those who are not true Christians in our days. These are also possible in those who are true Christians who are walking after their flesh rather than in the control of the Holy Spirit within them. May none of these faults and sins be a part of any of the lives of genuine Christians in our present times! Here are some definitions of these faults.

1. Paul And Titus Were Once Foolish.

THE MEANING OF THE GREEK WORD, ANOETAS

The Greek Word for "*foolish*" is ANOETAS. Some of the meanings of this Greek Word are:

"*1) not understood, unintelligible; 2) not understanding, unwise, foolish.*"

2. Paul And Titus Were Once Disobedient.

THE MEANING OF THE GREEK WORD, APEITHES

The Greek Word for "*disobedient*" is APEITHES. Some of the meanings of this Greek Word are:

"*1) impersuasible, not compliant, disobedient, contumacious.*"

3. Paul And Titus Were Once Deceived.

THE MEANING OF THE GREEK WORD, PLANAO

The Greek Word for "*deceived*" is PLANAO. This Greek verb is in the Greek present tense which indicates a continuous state or action. Some of the meanings of this Greek Word are:

"*1) to cause to stray, to lead astray, lead aside from the right way; 1a) to go astray, wander, roam about; metaph. 2a) to lead*

> *away from the truth, to lead into error, to deceive; 2b) to be led into error; 2c) to be led aside from the path of virtue, to go astray, sin; 2d) to sever or fall away from the truth; 2d1) of heretics; 2e) to be led away into error and sin."*

4. <u>Paul And Titus Were Once Serving Various Lusts And Pleasures.</u>

THE MEANING OF THE GREEK WORD, DOULEUO

The Greek Word for *"serving"* is DOULEUO. It is in the Greek present tense meaning it was a continuous action of serving. Some of the meanings of this Greek Word are:

> *"1) to be a slave, serve, do service; 1a) of a nation in subjection to other nations; 2) metaph. to obey, submit to; 2a) in a good sense, to yield obedience; 2b) in a bad sense, of those who become slaves to some base power, to yield to, give one's self up to."*

Here are the two things Paul and Titus were serving in time past before they became genuine Christians.

THE MEANING OF THE GREEK WORD, EPITHUMIA

The Greek Word for *"lusts"* is EPITHUMIA. Some of the meanings of this Greek Word are:

> *"1) desire, craving, longing, desire for what is forbidden, lust."*

THE MEANING OF THE GREEK WORD, HEDONE

The Greek Word for *"pleasures"* is HEDONE. Some of the meanings of this Greek Word are:

> *"1) pleasure; 2) desires for pleasure"*

This is much the same meaning we have in English. Our English word *"hedonism"* comes from this Greek Word.

Some of the English definitions of *"hedonism"* that make clear what this concept means to us today:

> *"the pursuit of pleasure; sensual*

> *self-indulgence; self-indulgence, pleasure-seeking, self-gratification, lotus-eating, sybaritism, intemperance, immodertion, extravagance, luxury, high living."*

This desire for pleasure is brought on today, among other things, by the use of various drugs. One city, mentioned on the Internet as this is being written, had **49,714 reported deaths due to drugs**.

5. <u>Paul And Titus Were Once Living In Malice And Envy.</u>

THE MEANING OF THE GREEK WORD, DIAGO

The Greek Word for *"living"* (DIAGO) is in the Greek Present tense. It indicates continuous actions in these two sins.

THE MEANING OF THE GREEK WORD, KAKIA

The Greek Word for *"malice"* is KAKIA. Some of the meanings of that Greek Word are:

> *"1) malignity, malice, ill-will, desire to injure; 2) wickedness, depravity; 2a) wickedness that is not ashamed to break laws; 3) evil, trouble."*

THE MEANING OF THE GREEK WORD, PHTHONOS

The Greek Word for *"envy"* is PHTHONOS. Some of the meanings of this Greek Word are:

> *"1) envy; 2) for envy, i.e. prompted by envy."*

Some of meanings of this English word are:

> *"a feeling of discontented or resentful longing aroused by someone else's possessions, qualities, or luck; synonyms: jealousy, covetousness, resentment, bitterness, discontent, the green-eyed monster."*

6. Paul And Titus Were Once Hateful And Hating One Another.

Paul and Titus were formerly not only "hateful," but also "*hating one another*." That Greek verb is in the Greek present tense which means that being hateful was a continuous action.

THE MEANING OF THE GREEK WORD, MISEO

The Greek Word for "*hating*" is MISEO. Some of the meanings of this Greek Word are:

"*1) to hate, pursue with hatred, detest; 2) to be hated, detested.*"

Every one of these above sins of the flesh are serious, especially when the Apostle Paul and Pastor Timothy are included in those who practiced them formerly before they became genuine Christians. Only by God's saving grace and power can true Christians today escape falling into the same evils through a moment by moment walk in the power and control of God the Holy Spirit Who indwells them.

Titus 3:4

"But after that the kindness and love of God our Saviour toward man appeared,"

Now, Paul tells Pastor Titus what happened after he had been living a sinful and wicked life as a Jewish Pharisee for many decades. This change was made by the appearing to him of the God and Saviour, the Lord Jesus Christ.

The Saviour appeared to Paul on his way to Damascus where he was going to imprison and perhaps kill Christians. The Lord appeared to him in His kindness and love in order to save his soul and give him a commission to preach Christ's gospel to many. Paul was receptive and obedient to Christ's call and commission.

Verses On Kindness

- **Psalms 117:2**

"For his merciful kindness is great toward us: and the truth of the LORD *endureth* for ever. Praise ye the LORD."

All people should be happy that God's merciful kindness is great toward sinners such as we are.

- **Ephesians 2:7**

"That in the ages to come he might shew the exceeding riches of his grace in *his* kindness toward us through Christ Jesus."

God manifested His kindness toward all the sinners who ever lived through sending His beloved Son into the world to die for everyone's sins and offer them eternal life by truly trusting Him.
- **Colossians 3:12**
"Put on therefore, as the elect of God, holy and beloved, bowels of mercies, kindness, humbleness of mind, meekness, longsuffering;"

Kindness and all these other attributes should be put on by genuine Christians as they live their daily lives, empowered by God the Holy Spirit Who indwells them.

Titus 3:5

"Not by works of righteousness which we have done, but according to his mercy he saved us, by the washing of regeneration, and renewing of the Holy Ghost;"

Nobody can be saved by their good works. It is only by God's mercy and regeneration by the work of the Holy Spirit. Let's go over some verses on these subjects.

Verses Against Being Saved By Our Works
- **Galatians 2:16**
"Knowing that a man is not justified by the works of the law, but by the faith of Jesus Christ, even we have believed in Jesus Christ, that we might be justified by the faith of Christ, and not by the works of the law: for by the works of the law shall no flesh be justified."

ONLY FAITH IN CHRIST CAN SAVE–NOT GOOD WORKS!

It is impossible for anyone to be saved by their own good works. Salvation comes to people only by their being justified by genuine faith in the Lord Jesus Christ as their Saviour.

- **Ephesians 2:8-9**
"For by grace are ye saved through faith; and that not of yourselves: *it is* the gift of God: Not of works, lest any man should boast. For we are his workmanship, created in Christ Jesus unto good works, which God hath before ordained that we should walk in them."

If people were saved by their good works, they might be able to boast about themselves. Good works please God after people are saved, but not before.

Verses On Mercy

God's mercy is the opposite of God's grace. Dr. M. R. DeHaan, Founder and Teacher of *THE RADIO BIBLE CLASS* in Grand Rapids, Michigan, gave a very good definition of these two words. In his Detroit Bible Class, years ago, I heard him say words to this effect:

THE CONTRASTS OF GOD'S "GRACE" AND "MERCY"

"Grace is getting something that we don't deserve. Mercy is not getting something that we do deserve."

I appreciate that definition, and have used it for many years.

- **Romans 11:32**

"For God hath concluded them all in unbelief, that he might have mercy upon all."

God concluded all Israel in unbelief so He could show His mercy on them all.

- **Romans 15:9**

"And that the Gentiles might glorify God for *his* mercy; as it is written, For this cause I will confess to thee among the Gentiles, and sing unto thy name."

All people should glorify God for His mercy which would be shown them if they receive the Lord Jesus Christ as their Saviour.

- **Ephesians 2:4**

"But God, who is rich in mercy, for his great love wherewith he loved us,"

GOD SHOWED HIS MERCY IN SENDING HIS SON

God's mercy is rich and abundant because of His love and sending His Son to die for the sins of the world so that those who believe on Him might have everlasting life.

- **1 Timothy 1:13**

"Who was before a blasphemer, and a persecutor, and injurious: but I obtained mercy, because I did *it* ignorantly in unbelief."

Paul was a great sinner, but when he accepted the Lord Jesus Christ as His Saviour, he received God's mercy and forgiveness.

- **1 Timothy 1:15-16**

"This *is* a faithful saying, and worthy of all acceptation, that Christ Jesus came into the world to save sinners; of whom I am chief. Howbeit for this cause <u>I obtained mercy</u>, that in me first Jesus Christ might shew forth all longsuffering, for a pattern to them which should hereafter believe on him to life everlasting."

That's why God saved Paul, to be a pattern to others who would be saved.

- **1 Peter 1:3**

"Blessed *be* the God and Father of our Lord Jesus Christ, which <u>according to his abundant mercy</u> hath begotten us again unto a lively hope by the resurrection of Jesus Christ from the dead,"

God's mercy is abundant and unending. We should be very thankful for this.

Verses On Regeneration Or A New Birth

- **John 1:10-13**

"He was in the world, and the world was made by him, and the world knew him not. He came unto his own, and his own received him not. But as many as received him, to them gave he power to become the sons of God, *even* to <u>them that believe on his name: Which were born</u>, not of blood, nor of the will of the flesh, nor of the will of man, but <u>of God</u>."

Being born-again by genuine faith in the Lord Jesus Christ is regeneration. That's the only way that anyone can get eternal life.

- **John 3:3**

"Jesus answered and said unto him, Verily, verily, I say unto thee, <u>Except a man be born again</u>, he cannot see the kingdom of God."

Being born-again is regeneration. That's the only way people can be a member of God's eternal family.

- **1 Peter 1:23**

"<u>Being born again</u>, not of corruptible seed, but of incorruptible, <u>by the word of God</u>, which liveth and abideth for ever."

> **GOD'S HEBREW AND GREEK WORDS ARE PRESERVED**
> Being born-again comes only by following the requirements laid down in the Words of God. The incorruptible and preserved Words of God refers to the original Hebrew, Aramaic, and Greek Words. These are the Words that underlie and have been accurately translated in the King James Bible.

- 1 John 5:1

"Whosoever <u>believeth that Jesus is the Christ is born of God</u>: and every one that loveth him that begat loveth him also that is begotten of him."

This is the means of regeneration and being born of God. True belief in the Lord Jesus Christ as the Saviour as their Saviour brings regeneration.

Titus 3:6

"Which he shed on us abundantly through Jesus Christ our Saviour;"

This verse goes back to Verse 5 which speaks about the renewing of the Holy Spirit. God the Holy Spirit has been abundantly shed upon and indwells all born-again regenerated genuine Christians who have been saved by truly trusting the Lord Jesus Christ as their Saviour.

Verses On God The Holy Spirit

- Acts 2:33

"Therefore being by the right hand of God exalted, and <u>having received of the Father the promise of the Holy Ghost</u>, he hath shed forth this, which ye now see and hear."

On the Day of Pentecost, God sent His Holy Spirit upon the genuine Christians that were meeting at that feast.

- Romans 5:5

"And hope maketh not ashamed; because <u>the love of God is shed abroad in our hearts by the Holy Ghost which is given unto us</u>."

God the Father has provided His love by the Holy Spirit Who indwells all true Christians.

- 1 Corinthians 6:19-20

"What? know ye not that <u>your body is the temple of the Holy Ghost *which is* in you</u>, which ye have of God, and ye are not your own? For ye are bought with a price: therefore glorify God in your body, and in your spirit, which are God's."

It is clear from this verse that the Holy Spirit indwells the bodies of all true Christians.
- **Galatians 5:22-23**
"But the fruit of the Spirit is love, joy, peace, longsuffering, gentleness, goodness, faith, meekness, temperance: against such there is no law."

> **GODLY CHRISTIANS CAN SHOW THESE NINE FRUITS**
> All nine fruits of the Holy Spirit are listed here. If genuine Christians are led and controlled by the Spirit, these fruits will be manifested.

- **2 Timothy 1:14**
"That good thing which was committed unto thee keep by the Holy Ghost which dwelleth in us."

God the Holy Spirit indwells all genuine Christians.
- **James 4:5**
"Do ye think that the scripture saith in vain, The spirit that dwelleth in us lusteth to envy?"

The indwelling Holy Spirit wants all true Christians to follow His leading. If this does not happen, He will be envious of the Christians following the false leading instead of His leading.
- **2 Corinthians 1:22**
"Who hath also sealed us, and given the earnest of the Spirit in our hearts."

The Holy Spirit Who indwells all genuine Christians is an "earnest" or a down-payment showing that they will one day receive their glorified bodies by the Holy Spirit's power.
- **Ephesians 1:13**
"In whom ye also *trusted*, after that ye heard the word of truth, the gospel of your salvation: in whom also after that ye believed, ye were sealed with that holy Spirit of promise,"

God the Holy Spirit has sealed all genuine Christians. This means they will be saved eternally. His seal can never be broken.
- **Ephesians 4:30**
"And grieve not the holy Spirit of God, whereby ye are sealed unto the day of redemption."

> **CHRISTIANS SHOULD NOT GRIEVE THE HOLY SPIRIT**
> True Christians are to stop grieving the Holy Spirit whereby they are sealed until their redemption. Some have taught, and I agree with them, that known and unconfessed sin in the life of genuine Christians is what grieves the Holy Spirit.

Titus 3:7

"That being justified by his grace, we should be made heirs according to the hope of eternal life."

All who are genuine Christians have been justified by God's grace and thus made the possessors of eternal life. This justification is not by any kind of works that people might do. Good works should follow salvation, but not be done to attain everlasting life. Everlasting life is given to true Christians by their true faith in the Lord Jesus Christ as their Saviour.

Verses On Being Justified

- **Acts 13:39**

"And <u>by him all that believe are justified from all things</u>, from which ye could not be justified by the law of Moses."

By genuine faith in the Lord Jesus Christ, true Christians are justified by Him. from all things. This justification could never come by following the Old Testament law of Moses.

- **Romans 3:24**

"<u>Being justified</u> freely by his grace <u>through the redemption</u> that is <u>in Christ Jesus</u>:"

Justification before God is made possible only to those who have availed themselves of the redemption that is in the Lord Jesus Christ.

- **Romans 3:28**

"Therefore we conclude that a <u>man is justified by faith without the deeds of the law</u>."

- **Romans 5:1**

"Therefore <u>being justified by faith, we have peace with God</u> through our Lord Jesus Christ:"

> **JUSTIFICATION IS ONLY BY TRUE FAITH IN CHRIST**
> Being justified in the eyes of God comes by genuine faith in the Lord Jesus Christ. This brings peace with God. It is <u>not attained by any good works a person might perform.</u>

- **Romans 5:9**
"Much more then, <u>being now justified by his blood</u>, we shall be saved from wrath through him."
Bible justification is based only on Christ's sacrifice of His blood on the cross. If justified by God, all true Christians will be saved from the wrath of the Tribulation period and from the wrath of Hell.
- **Romans 3:24**
"Being <u>justified freely by his grace through the redemption that is in Christ Jesus</u>:"
Justification is only through the redemption provided by the Lord Jesus Christ.

Verses On Grace

- **2 Corinthians 8:9**
"For ye know <u>the grace of our Lord Jesus Christ</u>, that, though he was rich, yet for your sakes he became poor, that ye through his poverty might be rich."
The grace of the Lord Jesus Christ was powerful. He was rich in Heaven, but became poor by coming to this wicked world and dying for the sins of the world on Calvary's cross. It is truly "getting something no one in this world deserves.
- **Ephesians 1:7**
"In whom we have redemption through his blood, the forgiveness of sins, <u>according to the riches of his grace</u>;"
God's grace brought the Lord Jesus Christ to be sacrificed on Calvary's cross to offer redemption to those who receive the Saviour.
- **Ephesians 2:8**
"For <u>by grace are ye saved</u> through faith; and that not of yourselves: *it is* the gift of God:"
Only by God's grace is it possible to be saved through faith in the Saviour.
- **Titus 2:11**
"For <u>the grace of God that bringeth salvation</u> hath appeared to all men,"
God's grace brought the provision of eternal salvation for those who properly receive it through the Saviour.

Verses On Heirs

- **Romans 8:17**
"And <u>if children, then heirs; heirs of God, and joint-heirs with Christ</u>; if so be that we suffer with *him*, that we may be also glorified together."

> **TRUE CHRISTIANS ARE JOINT HEIRS WITH CHRIST**
> People who are children of God by genuine faith in the Lord Jesus Christ are heirs of God and join-heirs with Christ.

- **Galatians 3:29**

"And if ye *be* Christ's, then are ye Abraham's seed, and <u>heirs according to the promise</u>."

All those who belong to the Lord Jesus Christ are made heirs according to God's promises.

- **Hebrews 1:14**

"Are they not all ministering spirits, sent forth to minister for them who shall be <u>heirs of salvation</u>?"

All genuine Christians who are heirs of salvation have ministering angels to help them during their lifetime. They assist in many ways, though unseen.

- **James 2:5**

"Hearken, my beloved brethren, Hath not God chosen the poor of this world rich in faith, and <u>heirs of the kingdom which he hath promised to them that love him</u>?"

God has chosen mainly the poor of this world to be heirs of His kingdom in Heaven. Though there might be a few who are rich, most of them are, by comparison, poor in this world, but rich in faith.

Titus 3:8

"This is a faithful saying, and these things I will that thou affirm constantly, that they which have believed in God might be careful to maintain good works. These things are good and profitable unto men."

The thing that Paul told Pastor Titus in this verse was so faithful and true that he wanted him to affirm it constantly.

> **MEANING OF THE GREEK WORD, DIABEBAIOOMAI**
> The Greek Word for *"constantly"* is DIABEBAIOOMAI. Some of the meanings of this Greek Word are:
> *"1) to affirm strongly, assert confidently."*
> Since this Greek verb is in the Greek present tense, it means that this action should be done continuously.

This action was to be applied to those genuine Christians who were in the church in Crete where Titus was the Pastor. He was not to apply this to non-Christians. These true Christians were to be careful to maintain good works.

THE MEANING OF THE GREEK WORD, PHRONTIZO

The Greek Word for "*be careful*" is PHRONTIZO. Some of the meanings of this Greek Word are:

"*1) to think, to be careful; 2) to be thoughtful or anxious.*"

Since this Greek verb is in the Greek present tense, it means that these genuine Christians were to be continuously thoughtful and anxious regarding these good works.

THE MEANING OF THE GREEK WORD, PROISTEMI

The Greek Word for "*maintain*" is PROISTEMI. Some of the meanings of this Greek Word are:

"*1) to set or place before; 1a) to set over; 1b) to be over, to superintend, preside over; 1c) to be a protector or guardian; 1c1) to give aid; 1d) to care for, give attention to; 1d1) profess honest occupations.*"

This verb is also in the Greek present tense which emphasized that this maintaining should be done continuously.

The reason why Pastor Timothy was to be eager to affirm continuously this statement about good works was because these good works were good and profitable unto those who witnessed them.

THE BIBLE IS THE STANDARD FOR "GOOD WORKS"

The only standard by which to judge whether "*works*" are "*good*" is the standard of the Words of God. Many works, deeds, or actions performed by people today are thought by them to be "*good*" and all right. However, the world's standards of "*good*," if they are in contradiction to God's standards, are "*bad*" rather than "*good*."

Verses On Good Works
- **Matthew 5:16**

"<u>Let your light so shine</u> before men, <u>that they may see your good works</u>, and glorify your Father which is in heaven."

The Lord Jesus Christ told His disciples that their light was to so shine that people might see their good works and glorify God Who is in Heaven. This should be done by genuine Christians today as well.

- **Acts 9:36**

"Now there was at Joppa a certain disciple named <u>Tabitha</u>, which by interpretation is called <u>Dorcas</u>: this woman <u>was full of good works</u> and almsdeeds which she did."

This woman had trusted the Lord Jesus Christ as her Saviour and had many good works which others were able to see.

- **Ephesians 2:10**

"For we are his workmanship, <u>created in Christ Jesus unto good works</u>, which God hath before ordained that <u>we should walk in them</u>."

GOOD WORKS SHOULD FOLLOW SALVATION

Paul is speaking to those who are true Christians saved by true faith in the Lord Jesus Christ. After they were saved, they should walk in good works as a testimony to others.

Verses On Christian Women And Good Works
- **1 Timothy 2:10**

"But (which <u>becometh women professing godliness</u>) with <u>good works</u>."

Women professing godliness who are genuine Christians were to perform good works.

- **1 Timothy 5:10**

"<u>Well reported of for good works</u>; if she have brought up children, if she have lodged strangers, if she have washed the saints' feet, if she have relieved the afflicted, <u>if she have diligently followed every good work</u>."

These were the standards that widows had to maintain before the local churches could assist them. They had to be "*well reported of for good works.*"

- **1 Timothy 6:18**

"That they do good, <u>that they be rich in good works</u>, ready to distribute, willing to communicate;"

Those true Christians who are rich should not only be rich in worldly goods, but also rich in good and helpful works for those in need.
- **2 Timothy 3:17**
"That the man of God may be perfect, throughly furnished unto all good works."

> **BIBLE STUDY NEEDED TO FIND GOOD WORKS**
> This is why genuine Christians should read, study, and know their Bibles so that they may be *"throughly furnished unto all good works."*

- **Titus 2:7**
"In all things shewing thyself a pattern of good works: in doctrine *shewing* uncorruptness, gravity, sincerity,"

The true Christian young men and women in Bible-believing churches should be a pattern of good works for others to see and follow.

- **Titus 2:14**
"Who gave himself for us, that he might redeem us from all iniquity, and purify unto himself a peculiar people, zealous of good works."

The Lord Jesus Christ gave Himself on the cross of Calvary dying for the sins of all the people in the world. His purpose was to redeem from iniquity those who accept Him as their Saviour. He wanted these people to be a peculiar people who are zealous of good works.

- **Hebrews 10:24**
"And let us consider one another to provoke unto love and to good works:"

- **1 Peter 2:12**
"Having your conversation honest among the Gentiles: that, whereas they speak against you as evildoers, they may by your good works, which they shall behold, glorify God in the day of visitation."

Peter is writing to former Jews who had become genuine Christians. He told them that their fruitful good works, beheld by many, might be used to glorify God.

Titus 3:9

"But avoid foolish questions, and genealogies, and contentions, and strivings about the law; for they are unprofitable and vain."

Genuine Christians are to avoid foolish questions, genealogies, contentions, and strivings.

> **THE MEANING OF THE GREEK WORD, PERIISTEMI**
>
> The Greek Word for "*avoid*" is PERIISTEMI. Some of the meanings of this Greek Word are:
>
>> "*1) to place around one; 2) to stand around; 2a) to turn one's self about for the purpose of avoiding something; 2b) to avoid, shun.*"
>
> Since this verb is in the Greek present tense, it means to avoid all the time and continuously.

These foolish questions might be Godless or stupid. True Christians are to avoid any of these without even trying to answer them.

The concern for genealogies are also to be avoided. The Mormon church stresses some of these things as do people who are trying to prove that all people are somehow connected to the Jewish race or some other race.

Contentions and strivings about the law of Moses are also to be avoided.

> **THE MEANING OF THE GREEK WORD, ERIS**
>
> The Greek Word for "*contentions*" is ERIS. Some of the meanings of that Greek Word are:
>
>> "*1) contention, strife, wrangling.*"

> **THE MEANING OF THE GREEK WORD, MACHE**
>
> The Greek Word for "*strivings*" is MACHE. Some of the meanings of that Greek Word are:
>
>> "*1) a fight or combat; 1a) of those in arms, a battle; 1b) of persons at variance, disputants etc., strife, contention; 1c) a quarrel.*"

The two reasons why all four of the things listed in this verse are to be avoided is that they are all both (1) unprofitable, and (2) vain.

THE MEANING OF THE GREEK WORD, ANOPOHELES

The Greek Word for "*unprofitable*" is ANOPHELES. Some of the meanings of this Greek Word are:

"*1) unprofitable; useless.*"

THE MEANING OF THE GREEK WORD, MATAIOS

The Greek Word for "*vain*" is MATAIOS. Some of the meanings of this Greek Word are:

"*1) devoid of force, truth, success, result;
2) useless, of no purpose.*"

Genuine Christians are often tempted to engage in some of the foolish questions that non-Christians like to throw at them. Though it is very tempting to spend many minutes attempting to answer such questions, the true Christians should decide if the questions are "foolish" or otherwise. If they are indeed "foolish," they should be avoided. No attempt should be made to answer them.

Verses On Unprofitable

- **Luke 17:10**

"So likewise ye, when ye shall have done all those things which are commanded you, say, We are unprofitable servants: we have done that which was our duty to do."

The Lord Jesus Christ told His disciples that if they did only what things that were commanded of them and no more, they should agree that they were unprofitable servants. The Lord wants true Christians to go above and beyond the minimum that is required of them.

- **Romans 3:12**

"They are all gone out of the way, they are together become unprofitable; there is none that doeth good, no, not one."

It's talking about the heathen world, the wicked, sinful world. There's not anyone that does good, not one. Every person who ever lived was born a sinner before God. Only genuine salvation by genuine faith in the Lord Jesus Christ can bring redemption and salvation from sin's penalty of eternal death in Hell.

- **Philemon 1:11**

"Which in time past was to thee unprofitable, but now profitable to thee and to me:"

Onesimus was a slave and unprofitable to the slave master, Philemon, until Paul led him to the Saviour.

Titus 3:10

"A man that is an heretick after the first and second admonition reject;"

The Apostle Paul warns Pastor Titus about heretics and how to deal with them.

THE MEANING OF THE GREEK WORD, HAIRETIKOS

The Greek Word for *"heretic"* is HAIRETIKOS. Some of the meanings of that Greek Word are:

*"1) fitted or able to take or choose a thing;
2) schismatic, factious, a follower of a false doctrine; 3) heretic."*

THE ORIGIN OF "HAIRETIKOS"

HAIRETIKOS comes from the verb, HAIREO, which means *"to choose."* In this case the *"heretic"* has chosen something that is contrary to the Words of God clearly found in the Hebrew, Aramaic, and Greek Words as originally written and preserved to this day in the Traditional Texts of the Bible. These preserved Words have been accurately translated in the King James Bible. A heretic is a person who accepts some Biblical heresy or false teaching.

Heresies or false teachings cover many things. Here are just a few of the many Biblical heresies in order to give the reader an understanding of what this verse is referring to. I'll just list the first **15 heresies** that come to mind as I am writing this:

1. Heresy #1–The denial of the Biblical creation of the world, man, animals and all other things.
2. Heresy #2–The denial of the inerrancy and infallibility of God's preserved Hebrew, Aramaic, and Greek Words of the Bible.
3. Heresy #3–The denial of the virgin birth of the Lord Jesus Christ.
4. Heresy #4–The denial of Christ's many miracles.
5. Heresy #5–The denial of Christ's eternal existence.
6. Heresy #6–The denial of Christ's incarnation.

7. Heresy #7–The denial of Christ's Deity.
8. Heresy #8–The denial of Christ's bodily resurrection.
9. Heresy #9–The denial of Christ's bodily ascension into Heaven.
10. Heresy #10–The denial of Christ's presence in Heaven now.
11. Heresy #11–The denial that Christ died for the sins of the entire world.
12. Heresy #12–The denial that all people are sinners in the eyes of God.
13. Heresy #13–The denial that good works of any kind cannot bring anyone forgiveness and salvation.
14. Heresy #14–The denial that whoever truly believes that the Lord Jesus Christ died for them can be forgiven of their sins and be given the gift of eternal life.
15. Heresy #15–The denial that there is a literal and eternal Hell with literal fire where every non-Christian will spend eternity, etc., etc.

This verse teaches that, after there has been a discussion with a person about their Biblical beliefs, and they are found to hold some Biblical heresies and are therefore heretics, they should be rejected.

THE MEANING OF THE GREEK WORD, PARAITEOMAI

The Greek Word for *"rejected"* is PARAITEOMAI. Some of the meanings of this Greek Word are:

> *"1) to ask along side, beg to have near one; 1a) to obtain by entreaty; 1b) to beg from, to ask for, supplicate; 2) to avert by entreaty or seek to avert, to deprecate; 2a) to entreat that ... not; 2b) to refuse, decline 2c) to shun, avoid; 2d) to avert displeasure by entreaty; 2d1) to beg pardon, crave indulgence, to excuse; 2d2) of one excusing himself for not accepting a wedding; invitation to a feast."*

BIBLICAL SEPARATION FROM HERETICS NEEDED

In view of this verse, there should be Biblical separation from all heresies and heretics who believe them. The breakdown in such separation has led to compromise and apostasy in all Protestant denominations.

- **Romans 16:17**
  "Now I beseech you, brethren, <u>mark them which cause divisions</u> and offences <u>contrary to the doctrine</u> which ye have learned; <u>and avoid them</u>."

Two things should take place when genuine Christians see people who hold to divisions contrary to Biblical doctrine.
1. First, they should be "*marked*" (clearly and publicly pointed out) and exposed.
2. Second, they should be "*avoided.*"

Titus 3:11

"Knowing that he that is such is subverted, and sinneth, being condemned of himself."

These heretics referred to in the preceding verse are subverted and are condemned of themselves

---

THE MEANING OF THE GREEK WORD, EXSTREPHO

The Greek Word for "subverted" is EXSTREPHO. Some of the meanings of this Greek Word are:

"*1) to turn or twist out, tear up; 2) to turn inside out, invert; 3) to change for the worse, pervert, corrupt.*"

PASTORS SHOULD CALL FOR BIBLICAL SEPARATION

No wonder God clearly tells true Christians to avoid and separate from such heretics. They should be both rejected and avoided. Pastors should speak out and expose false and apostate doctrines as taught by apostates, neo-evangelicals, and even some Fundamentalists (sad to say.)

Titus 3:12

"When I shall send Artemas unto thee, or Tychicus, be diligent to come unto me to Nicopolis: for I have determined there to winter."

Paul mentioned two of his fellow-workers, Artemas and Tychicus. Artemas is only mentioned in this place in the Scriptures. Paul was going to send either Artemas or Tychicus to Pastor Titus in Ephesus. Paul was going to spend the winter in Nicopolis.

Verses About Tychicus
- **Acts 20:4**

"And there accompanied him into Asia Sopater of Berea; and of the Thessalonians, Aristarchus and Secundus; and Gaius of Derbe, and Timotheus; and of Asia, Tychicus and Trophimus."

Tychicus accompanied Paul to Asia Minor (which is present-day Turkey).

- **Ephesians 6:21**

"But that ye also may know my affairs, *and* how I do, Tychicus, a beloved brother and faithful minister in the Lord, shall make known to you all things:"

From his Roman prison, Paul told the true Christians in Ephesus that he would send Tychicus to them to make known to them how Paul was doing in prison.

- **Colossians 4:7**

"All my state shall Tychicus declare unto you, *who is* a beloved brother, and a faithful minister and fellowservant in the Lord:"

Paul told the Christians at Colosse the same thing as he told those in Ephesus, namely, that Tychicus would fill them in about how he was doing in the Roman prison.

- **2 Timothy 4:12**

"And Tychicus have I sent to Ephesus."

Paul was in his second Roman imprisonment when he mentioned that he had sent Tychicus to Ephesus.

Titus 3:13

"Bring Zenas the lawyer and Apollos on their journey diligently, that nothing be wanting unto them."

Paul asked Pastor Titus to help Zenas and Apollos on their journey so they would have everything they needed.

Some Verses About Apollos
- **Acts 18:24**

"And a certain Jew named Apollos, born at Alexandria, an eloquent man, *and* mighty in the scriptures, came to Ephesus."

Apollos was eloquent and mighty in the Scriptures. These were gifts that the Lord was able to use.

- **1 Corinthians 16:12**

"As touching *our* brother Apollos, I greatly desired him to come unto you with the brethren: but his will was not at all to come at this time; but he will come when he shall have convenient time."

Paul wanted Apollos to come to the Corinthian church, but he didn't want to come at that time, but would come later at a convenient time.

Titus 3:14

"And let ours also learn to maintain good works for necessary uses, that they be not unfruitful."

Paul is mentioning to Pastor Titus that genuine Christians should learn to maintain good works after they are saved.

THE MEANING OF THE GREEK WORD, MANTHANO

The Greek Word for *"learn"* is MANTHANO. Some of the meanings of this Greek Word are:

> *"1) to learn, be appraised; 1a) to increase one's knowledge, to be increased in knowledge; 1b) to hear, be informed; 1c) to learn by use and practice; 1c1) to be in the habit of, accustomed to."*

This Greek verb is in the Greek present tense which means that this action of learning is to be continuous.

THE MEANING OF THE GREEK WORD, PROISTEMI

The Greek Word for *"maintain"* is PROISTEMI. Some of the meanings of this Greek Word are:

> *"1) to set or place before; 1a) to set over; 1b) to be over, to superintend, preside over; 1c) to be a protector or guardian; 1c1) to give aid; 1d) to care for, give attention to; 1d1) profess honest occupations."*

Paul mentions that Pastor Titus was to care for and give attention to these good works for *"necessary"* uses.

THE MEANING OF THE GREEK WORD, ANAGKAIOS

The Greek Word for *"necessary"* is ANAGKAIOS. Some of the meanings of this Greek Word are:

> *"1) necessary; 1a) what one can not do without, indispensable; 1b) connected by bonds of nature or friendship; 1c) what ought according to the law of duty be*

> *done, what is required by the circumstances."*

These good works are indispensable. Otherwise the genuine Christians would be unfruitful in their ministries.

THE MEANING OF THE GREEK WORD, AKARPOS

The Greek Word for *"unfruitful"* is AKARPOS. Some of the meanings of this Greek Word are:

"1) metaph. without fruit, barren, not yielding what it ought to yield."

True Christians who do not bear Godly fruit in their lives are not a light to the many non-Christians around them. These unsaved people need to see some light and good fruit in the lives of those who profess and possess the Christian faith.

Verses On Unfruitful
- **Matthew 13:22**

"He also that received seed among the thorns is he that heareth the word; and the care of this world, and the deceitfulness of riches, choke the word, and he becometh unfruitful."

In this illustration, given by the Lord Jesus Christ, worldly cares and deceitful riches choked God's Words and the person became an unfruitful person.

- **2 Peter 1:8**

"For if these things be in you, and abound, they make *you that ye shall* neither *be* barren nor unfruitful in the knowledge of our Lord Jesus Christ."

PRACTICING EIGHT VIRTUES BRINGS FRUITFULNESS

Peter has just listed eight virtues for true Christians to observe and follow. If they are followed, they will not be barren or unfruitful in the knowledge of their Saviour, the Lord Jesus Christ. (See 2 Peter 1:5-7 for these eight virtues.)

Titus 3:15

"All that are with me salute thee. Greet them that love us in the faith. Grace be with you all. Amen. "

Paul concludes his letter to Pastor Titus by sending him greetings from all who are with Paul at the time. He also asks Titus to greet all those around him in his church and others who love Paul in the faith.

He closes by sending his grace to Titus and his entire church on the island of Crete.

Paul finishes his letter with the word "Amen." This word has an interesting history and meaning. Let me give one of the historic definitions of this word:

> ### THE MEANING OF "AMEN"
> "*The word "amen" is a most remarkable word. It was transliterated directly from the Hebrew into the Greek of the New Testament, then into Latin and into English and many other languages, so that it is practically a universal word.* It has been called the best known word in human speech. The word is directly related -- in fact, almost identical -- to the Hebrew word for "believe" (amam), or faithful. *Thus, it came to mean "sure" or "truly", an expression of absolute trust and confidence.*"

INDEX OF WORDS AND PHRASES

1,000 years, the length of the Millennium 30
15 heresies held by many today. 106
356 doctrinal passages in the Gnostic Critical Greek Texts. ... 22, 55
356 doctrinal passages that contain false doctrines. 22
About the Author. iv
accurately translated in the King James Bible. 96, 106
Acknowledgments. .... ii, iv
Adam. 28
AFTER SALVATION--SERVANTS OF RIGHTEOUSNESS 59
all people are sinners in the eyes of God. 107
American Standard Version (ASV) based on Gnostic Texts. 4
An Important Verse On Godly. 69
ANDROS. 50
ANSWER QUESTIONS WITH MEEKNESS. 88
Antichrists. 29
ANTICHRISTS DENY CHRIST'S INCARNATION. 29
apostate Protestant church leaders. 35
Apostle Paul. 1, 2, 33, 39, 53, 54, 64, 78, 81, 88, 89, 92, 106
ASV (American Standard Version) based on Gnostic Texts. 22
barren. 111
Be Obedient To Their Own Husbands. 53
bestiality. 36
BFT #3488. 50
BFT #4166. I
BFT Phone: 856-854-4452. I
Bible For Today Baptist Church. .... I, iii, 24, 35
BIBLE STUDY NEEDED TO FIND GOOD WORKS 103
Biblical creation. 106
Biblical doctrines. 24, 34
Biblical heresies. 106, 107
Biblical pastor. 15, 16
Biblical separation from all heresies and heretics. 107
BIBLICAL SEPARATION FROM HERETICS NEEDED 107
Bill Hybels. 35
Billy Graham. 30
Blameless. 13-15, 17, 26, 36
Calvary. 7, 64, 72, 73, 103

Calvinists.. 63, 65, 73, 74
Canter, Patty, typed the rough draft and proofread the book..... iii
Christ died for the sins of the entire world..................... 107
CHRISTIAN EMPLOYERS SHOULD BE FAIR AND JUST...... 61
CHRISTIANS MUST NOT DECEIVE OR BE DECEIVED........ 27
CHRISTIANS SHOULD BE DEVOTED TO CHRIST.............. 1
CHRISTIANS SHOULD NOT BE TOSSED TO AND FRO........ 28
CHRISTIANS SHOULD HONOR THEIR EMPLOYERS......... 60
CHRISTIANS SHOULD LOOK TO THE SAVIOUR.............. 71
CHRISTIANS SHOULD NOT GRIEVE THE HOLY SPIRIT...... 98
Christ's bodily ascension into Heaven......................... 107
Christ's bodily resurrection................................... 107
Christ's Deity... 107
Christ's eternal existence..................................... 106
Christ's incarnation...................................... 29, 106
Christ's presence in Heaven now to interceded for Christians... 107
Church Phone: 856-854-4747 and 856-261-9018 (Pastor's cell)... I
compromising Bible-believing church leaders 35
craftiness... 28, 42
Crete................... 1, 8, 10, 11, 26, 41, 52, 54, 55, 101, 112
deceive.. 27-30, 42, 90
Defined King James Bible Orders............................ iv
Deny Ungodliness... 65
Deny Worldly Lusts.. 67
Devil... 28-30, 49, 67
divorce and re-marry... 14
doctrine............. 7, 22, 23, 25, 28, 32-34, 41-45, 48, 54, 55, 60,
                                           61, 75, 78, 103, 106, 108
doctrines............. 4, 7, 22-25, 31-35, 38, 41-44, 47, 61, 78, 108
DON'T ADMIT FALSE TEACHERS INTO YOUR HOUSE........ 44
employers.. 60, 61
ESV.. 22
eternal Hell with literal fire.................................. 107
Eve... 28
EVE WAS DECEIVED BY THE SATAN-SERPENT.............. 28
everlasting Hell.. 66
e-mail: BFT@BibleForToday.org................................ I
Faithful Children....................................... 13, 14, 26
faithful Words.. 22, 25
FAITHFUL WORDS MUST BE PASSED ON..................... 25
false Bible versions...................................... 52, 55

false English versions. 22
false Hebrew, Aramaic, and Gnostic critical Greek texts 22
false teachers. 30-32, 44
FALSE TEACHERS' MOTIVE--FILTHY LUCRE.. 31
FAX: 856-854-2464.. I
female. 36
fifteen Biblical qualifications. 13, 22
FIRM IN DEFENDING GOD'S WORDS, BUT GENTLE 87
foolish questions. 104, 105
Foreword.. .... iii, iv
fornication.. .... 52, 67
Four Verses On Sound Doctrine. 44
genealogies. 104
genuine Christians............... iii, 1, 2, 23, 27, 28, 33-38, 42-44,
               59-61, 63-70, 72, 74, 75, 83, 84, 86-90, 92,
               93, 96-98, 100-105, 108, 110, 111
GENUINE TRUST IN CHRIST GIVES ETERNAL LIFE 3
glorious appearing of the Lord Jesus Christ.. .... 2, 69, 70
Gnostic, their doctrinal heresies. 4, 22, 52, 55
Gnostic and Critical Greek Texts, the basis of modern versions. . . 55
Gnostic Critical Greek the false basis of modern versions. . . 4, 22, 55
GNOSTIC GREEK TEXT DOCTRINAL PERVERSIONS 55
GOD HATES UNGODLINESS AND JUDGES IT. 66
GOD SHOWED HIS MERCY IN SENDING HIS SON 94
GODLY CHRISTIANS CAN SHOW THESE NINE FRUITS 97
God's grace. 62-70, 94, 98, 99
God's Grace Teaches Us To Live Godly.. 69
God's Grace Teaches Us To Live Righteously.. 69
God's Grace Teaches Us To Live Soberly. 68
God's Name in vain, very, very common today. 69
GOOD WORKS SHOULD FOLLOW SALVATION. 98, 102
gospel.. .... 2, 4-7, 13, 22, 63-65, 84, 92, 97
grave. 17, 33, 45, 46
GUNE, a woman.. 50
He Must Be Holy, A qualification of a Biblical Pastor.. 21
He Must Be Just, A qualification of a Biblical Pastor. 20
He Must Be Sober, A qualification of a Biblical Pastor.. 20
He Must Be Temperate, A qualification of a Biblical Pastor. 21
Hebrew, Aramaic, and Greek Words.. .... 23, 35, 96, 106
Hell. 2, 6, 7, 30, 65, 66, 72, 99, 105, 107

Hell and its eternal fires. 7
heresies. 31, 106, 107
heretic. 25, 31, 32, 35, 55, 90, 106-108
heretical doctrines. 25, 31
heretical Greek words. 55
Hold Fast. 3, 22, 24, 28
Hollywood movies. 69
Holy Behavior.. 48
homosexual man. 14
homosexuality. 36, 50, 67
Husband Of One Wife, qualification of a Biblical Pastor.13, 14, 17, 26
Husband-Loving Lessons. 50
hyper Calvinists. 63
In Line With Sound Doctrine. 45, 48
Incarnation of the Lord Jesus Christ. 29, 106
Index of Words and Phrases. . . . . iii, iv, 113
Joel Osteen, a false teacher in many areas. 35
John 3:16-18. . . . . 73, 74
Judas Iscariot. 13
JUSTIFICATION IS ONLY BY TRUE FAITH IN CHRIST 98
Keepers At Home, a standard for Christian women. 51, 52
King James Bible. . . . . I, iii, iv, 1, 2, 19, 22, 35, 96, 106
KNOW DOCTRINE AND STAND FAST IN IT. 34
labor union. 57
Lake of Fire.. . . . . 2, 30, 65
Live So The Unbelievers Have No Evil Thing To Say 57
Lord Jesus Christ died for sinners.. 7
Love Their Children, a standard for Christian women. 50, 51
Lover Of Good Men, a qualification for a Biblical pastor. 19
Lover Of Hospitality, a qualification for a Biblical pastor. 19
male. 14, 36
MANY PREACHERS DO NOT PREACH GOD'S WORDS 7
MANY TODAY HOLD HERETICAL DOCTRINES. 25
mark them, the false teachers. 42, 108
masters or employers. 25, 57-61
Matthias, the wrong substitute for the Apostle Judas. 13
MEANING OF THE GREEK WORD, AISCHROKERDES 18
MEANING OF THE GREEK WORD, DIABEBAIOOMAI 100
MEANING OF THE GREEK WORD, KALODIDASKALOS 49
MEANING OF THE GREEK WORD, PHILAGATHAOS 19
MEANING OF THE GREEK WORD, PROSDECHOMAI 69

Mormon. 104
NASV, New American Standard Version. 22
NEPHALIOS, abstaining from alcoholic beverages. 16, 17
New American Standard Version (NASV). 4
New International Version (NIV). 4
NIV, New International Version. 22
NON-CHRISTIANS DESTINED TO HELL. 2
Not Be A Striker, a qualification for a Biblical pastor. 18
Not Be False Accusers, a qualification for older women.. 48
Not Be Given To Filthy Lucre, a qualification for a Biblical pastor. 18
Not Be Given To Much Wine, a qualification for older women.... 49
Not Be Given To Wine, a qualification for a Biblical pastor....... 16
Not Be Soon Angry, a qualification for a Biblical pastor. 15
Not Obeying If Laws Contradict The Bible..................... 83
NRSV, New Revised Standard Version........................ 22
Obama, Democratic President for 8 years, a Muslim. 3
ONLY FAITH IN CHRIST CAN SAVE–NOT GOOD WORKS!. ... 93
ordain, Titus was to ordain elders in every city............... 10-13
Order Blank Pages.. iv
Orders: 1-800-John 10:9. I
Other Verses On Masters. 60
OUR CHURCH CONTENDS EARNESTLY. 35
Pastor D. A. Waite. .... 1, I, iii
Pastor Timothy................ 7, 26, 33, 34, 37, 56, 60, 69, 88, 92,
101
PASTOR TIMOTHY WAS TO KEEP HIMSELF PURE 37
Pastor Titus.. .... 8, 23, 25, 31-33, 39, 45, 48, 53-57, 75, 76,
78, 81, 83, 85, 86, 89, 100, 106, 108-111
Pastor Titus Should Be A Pattern Of Good Works. 54
Pastor Titus Should Have Sound Speech That Can't Be
 Condemned. 56
Pastor Titus Should Have Uncorrupt Bible Doctrine 55
Pastor Titus Should Show Gravity............................ 56
Pastor Titus Should Show Sincerity. 56
PASTOR TITUS WAS TO REBUKE WITH AUTHORITY 33
pastor/bishop/elder, one office, three duties................. 10, 11
PASTORS ARE ORDAINED BY LOCAL CHURCHES 11
PASTORS MUST HOLD FAST ONLY FAITHFUL WORDS. 22
PASTORS MUST HOLD FAST TO GOD'S WORDS. 22
PASTORS MUST REPROVE WITH LONGSUFFERING......... 44
PASTORS SHOULD CALL FOR BIBLICAL SEPARATION...... 108

pastors/bishops/elders, one office, three duties. 10, 22, 43
Pastors-Bishops-Elders, one office, three duties. 13, 22, 23, 32
Patricia Canter, prepared the first draft and proofread finally. . . . iii
Paul And Titus Were Once Deceived. 89
Paul And Titus Were Once Disobedient. 89
Paul And Titus Were Once Foolish. 89
Paul And Titus Were Once Hateful. 92
Paul And Titus Were Once Living In Malice. 91
Paul And Titus Were Once Serving Various Lusts. 90
PAUL GREETS TITUS WITH GRACE, MERCY & PEACE. 8
PAUL WAS FAITHFUL TO CHRIST'S COMMISSION. 63
PERSECUTION SCATTERED THE CHRISTIANS. 5
PETER'S SELECTING MATTHIAS WAS IN ERROR. 13
polygamy, against New Testament Biblical doctrines. 36
PRACTICING EIGHT VIRTUES BRINGS FRUITFULNESS. 111
PREACHERS SHOULD BE CALLED BY GOD. 6
PREACHERS SHOULD PREACH BIBLE DOCTRINES. 4
PREACHING ABOUT THE CROSS IS NEEDED. 6
preserved Words, Hebrew and Greek Words under the KJB. 96, 106
President Obama, trained as a Communist and a Muslim. 3
prostitution, against Biblical doctrines. 52
rapture, Christ's pre-tribulation return for all true Christians. . 2, 70
RAPTURE POSITIONS–FIVE FALSE AND ONE TRUE. 70
rebuke, needed where Biblically proper. 7, 31-33, 43, 76-78
rebuke them sharply, false teacher. 31, 78
redeem, to receive salvation by true faith in Christ. 72, 75, 103
redemption, receive salvation by faith in Christ. . . 74, 75, 97-99, 105
Remind His Church Not To Be Brawlers, Pastor Titus was to. 86
Remind His Church To Be Gentle, Pastor Titus was to. 86
Remind His Church To Be Ready To Every Good Work, Pastor
       Titus was to. 85
Remind His Church To Be Subject To Principalities, Pastor
       Titus was to. 81
Remind His Church To Obey Magistrates, Pastor Titus was to. . . . 83
Remind His Church To Show Meekness To All People,
       Pastor Titus was to. 86
Remind His Church To Speak Evil Of No Man, Pastor
       Titus was to. 85
Revised Standard Version (RSV). 4
Rick Warren, a false teacher in many areas. 35
RIGHTEOUSNESS CAN'T COME BY MOSES' LAW. 64

Rome. 5, 42, 63, 67, 68
RSV, Revised Standard Version. 22
salvation. 9, 17, 35, 47, 59, 62-65, 74, 75, 88, 93, 97-100, 102, 105, 107
Satan. 28-30, 49
SATAN WILL BE CAST INTO HELL'S LAKE OF FIRE. 30
Saviour. 2-6, 8, 21, 30, 61-64, 69, 71, 74, 92-94, 96, 98, 99, 102, 103, 106, 111
Scripture. . . . . iii, 43, 97
Selfwilled, Biblical pastor not to be such. 14, 15
servants of God.. 59
set in order the things that were wanting. 10-12
SEVEN VERSES USING NEPHALIOS, no alcoholic drinks. 17
single man.. 14
Six Things For Aged Men. 45
sober. 17, 19, 20, 33, 45, 50, 53
Sodom, a city God destroyed because of their sins. 66
Some Verses On Apollos. 109
sound doctrine. 22, 23, 25, 33, 41, 44, 45, 48
Sound In Charity, a standard for Christian aged men. 47
Sound In Patience, a standard for Christian aged men. 47
Sound In The Faith, a standard for Christian aged men.. . . 31, 46, 78
sound Words and doctrines of God. 23
Steward Of God, a qualification for Biblical pastors. 14, 15
Table of Contents. iv
Teach The Young Women To Be Chaste. 51
Teach The Young Women To Be Good. 52
Teach The Young Women To Be Sober. 50
Teach The Young Women To Love Their Husbands. 50
Teachers Of Good Things. 48, 49
teachers' union, telling the employer what to do. 57
temperate, a Biblical trait for all to possess. . 17, 19-21, 33, 45, 46, 51
The Apostles Disobeyed Roman Orders. 84
THE APOSTLES OBEYED GOD RATHER THAN MAN. 84
THE APOSTLES PREACHED THE GOSPEL TO MANY. 5
THE BIBLE FOR TODAY PRESS. I
THE BIBLE IS THE STANDARD FOR "GOOD WORKS". 101
THE CONTRASTS OF GOD'S "GRACE" AND "MERCY". 94
THE CORINTHIAN CHURCH WAS DISORDERLY.. 12
THE CRETANS WERE TO BE REBUKED. 38
THE DANGERS OF SELF-DECEPTION. 27

THE EARLY CHURCH KEPT THE PROPER DOCTRINES. 42
the faith, doctrines with article. ... 1, 24, 31, 33-35, 37, 46, 78, 93, 111
THE GNOSTICS ACCEPTED MANY SEXUAL SINS. 52
THE MEANING OF THE GREEK WORD, ADIAPHTHORIA.. 55
THE MEANING OF THE GREEK WORD, ADOKIMOS. 38
THE MEANING OF THE GREEK WORD, AGAPE. 47
THE MEANING OF THE GREEK WORD, AGATHOS.. 52
THE MEANING OF THE GREEK WORD, AKARPOS........... 111
THE MEANING OF THE GREEK WORD, AMACHOS. 86
THE MEANING OF THE GREEK WORD, AMEOMAI. 66
THE MEANING OF THE GREEK WORD, ANAGKAIOS. 110
THE MEANING OF THE GREEK WORD, ANATREPO. 31
THE MEANING OF THE GREEK WORD, ANEGKLETOS....... 13
THE MEANING OF THE GREEK WORD, ANOETAS........... 89
THE MEANING OF THE GREEK WORD, ANOPOHELES.. 105
THE MEANING OF THE GREEK WORD, ANTILEGO....... 23, 58
THE MEANING OF THE GREEK WORD, ANUPOTAKTOS. 26
THE MEANING OF THE GREEK WORD, APHTHARSIA. 56
THE MEANING OF THE GREEK WORD, APOTOMOS......... 32
THE MEANING OF THE GREEK WORD, ARCHE. 82
THE MEANING OF THE GREEK WORD, AUTHADES. 15
THE MEANING OF THE GREEK WORD, BLASPHEMEO. 85
THE MEANING OF THE GREEK WORD, CHARIS.. 62
THE MEANING OF THE GREEK WORD, DIABOLOS.......... 48
THE MEANING OF THE GREEK WORD, DIAGO.. 91
THE MEANING OF THE GREEK WORD, DIDASKALIA........ 55
THE MEANING OF THE GREEK WORD, DIDOMI. 72
THE MEANING OF THE GREEK WORD, DIKAIOS............ 20
THE MEANING OF THE GREEK WORD, DOULEUO. 90
THE MEANING OF THE GREEK WORD, DOULOS............. 1, 57
THE MEANING OF THE GREEK WORD, ELEGCHO. ... 23, 31, 77
THE MEANING OF THE GREEK WORD, ENKRATES.. 21
THE MEANING OF THE GREEK WORD, EPIDIORTHOO...... 10
THE MEANING OF THE GREEK WORD, EPIEIKES........... 86
THE MEANING OF THE GREEK WORD, EPIPHAINO......... 62
THE MEANING OF THE GREEK WORD, EPISTOMIZO........ 30
THE MEANING OF THE GREEK WORD, EPITHUMIA.. ..... 67, 90
THE MEANING OF THE GREEK WORD, ERIS 104
THE MEANING OF THE GREEK WORD, EXOUSIA. 82
THE MEANING OF THE GREEK WORD, EXSTREPHO. 108

Titus Expounded Verse by Verse

THE MEANING OF THE GREEK WORD, HAGNOS............ 51
THE MEANING OF THE GREEK WORD, HAIRETIKOS....... 106
THE MEANING OF THE GREEK WORD, HEDONE............ 90
THE MEANING OF THE GREEK WORD, HIEROPREPES...... 48
THE MEANING OF THE GREEK WORD, HOSIOS............ 21
THE MEANING OF THE GREEK WORD, HUGIAINO....... 41, 46
THE MEANING OF THE GREEK WORD, HUGIES............ 56
THE MEANING OF THE GREEK WORD, HUPER............. 73
THE MEANING OF THE GREEK WORD, HUPOMENE......... 47
THE MEANING OF THE GREEK WORD, HUPOTASSO.. 53, 58, 81
THE MEANING OF THE GREEK WORD, KAKIA............. 91
THE MEANING OF THE GREEK WORD, KATHAROS......... 36
THE MEANING OF THE GREEK WORD, KATHISTEMI........ 11
THE MEANING OF THE GREEK WORD, KOSMEO............ 61
THE MEANING OF THE GREEK WORD, MACHE............ 104
THE MEANING OF THE GREEK WORD, MATAIOLOGOS...... 26
THE MEANING OF THE GREEK WORD, MATAIOS.......... 105
THE MEANING OF THE GREEK WORD, MISEO............. 92
THE MEANING OF THE GREEK WORD, NEPHALEOS......... 45
THE MEANING OF THE GREEK WORD, NOSPHIZOMAI...... 61
THE MEANING OF THE GREEK WORD, OIKONOMOS........ 15
THE MEANING OF THE GREEK WORD, OIKOUROS.......... 52
THE MEANING OF THE GREEK WORD, ORGILOS........... 15
THE MEANING OF THE GREEK WORD, PAIDEUO........... 65
THE MEANING OF THE GREEK WORD, PARAITEOMAI..... 107
THE MEANING OF THE GREEK WORD, PARAKALEO........ 76
THE MEANING OF THE GREEK WORD, PAROINOS.......... 16
THE MEANING OF THE GREEK WORD, PEITHARCHEO...... 83
THE MEANING OF THE GREEK WORD, PERIISTEMI....... 104
THE MEANING OF THE GREEK WORD, PERIOUSIOS........ 74
THE MEANING OF THE GREEK WORD, PERIPHONEO....... 77
THE MEANING OF THE GREEK WORD, PHAULOS........... 57
THE MEANING OF THE GREEK WORD, PHILANDROS....... 50
THE MEANING OF THE GREEK WORD, PHILOTEKNOS...... 51
THE MEANING OF THE GREEK WORD, PHILOXENOS....... 19
THE MEANING OF THE GREEK WORD, PHRENAPATES...... 26
THE MEANING OF THE GREEK WORD, PHRONTIZO....... 101
THE MEANING OF THE GREEK WORD, PHTHONOS.......... 91
THE MEANING OF THE GREEK WORD, PISTIS............ 46
THE MEANING OF THE GREEK WORD, PLANAO............ 89
THE MEANING OF THE GREEK WORD, PLEKTES........... 18

THE MEANING OF THE GREEK WORD, PRAOTES. 86
THE MEANING OF THE GREEK WORD, PREPO. 41
THE MEANING OF THE GREEK WORD, PROISTEMI. . . . 101, 110
THE MEANING OF THE GREEK WORD, SEMNOS. 46
THE MEANING OF THE GREEK WORD, SEMNOTES. 56
THE MEANING OF THE GREEK WORD, SOPHRON. . . . 20, 46, 51
THE MEANING OF THE GREEK WORD, SOPHRONEO. 53
THE MEANING OF THE GREEK WORD, SOPHRONIZO. 50
THE MEANING OF THE GREEK WORD, SOPHRONOS. 68
THE MEANING OF THE GREEK WORD, TUPOS. 54
THE MEANING OF THE GREEK WORD, ZELOTES. 74
THE MEANING OF "AMEN". 112
The Meaning Of "For," in our place for our benefit. 73
The Meaning Of "Us, the whole race of mankind. 73
THE OFFER OF ETERNAL LIFE. 2
THE ORIGIN OF "HAIRETIKOS". 106
THE PASTOR MUST HAVE FAITHFUL CHILDREN. 14
Titus Chapter One. iv
Titus Chapter Three. iv
Titus Chapter Two. iv
TITUS WAS PAUL'S HELPER. 9
TODAY'S PASTORS MUST MEET ALL 15 STANDARDS. 21
tormented day and night for ever, Hell's Lake of Fire. 30
TOTALLY ABSTAINING FROM ALCOHOL. 17
Traditional Greek Text--underlies the KJB's New Testament. 55
true Christians. 24, 27-29, 33, 34, 36, 37, 39, 43, 45, 59-
61, 64, 68-71, 74-76, 84-89, 92, 96-105,
108, 109, 111
true Hebrew, Aramaic, and Greek Words, underlying the KJB. . . . 23
Twelve Things For Aged Women. 48
universalism, a false doctrine. 63
Verses Against Being Saved By Our Works. 93
Verses On Authority. 78
Verses On Being Justified. 98
Verses On Christian Women. 102
Verses On Deceivers. 27
Verses On Doctrine. 42
Verses On Faithful. 25
Verses On Gentle. 87
Verses On God The Holy Spirit. 96
Verses On God's Promises. 3

Verses On Good Works. 75, 102
Verses On Grace. 63, 99
Verses On Heirs. 99
Verses On Hope. 2
Verses On Kindness. 92
Verses On Looking. 70
Verses On Lusts. 67
Verses On Meekness. 87
Verses On Mercy. 94
Verses On Ordain. 12
Verses On Preaching. 4
Verses On Pure. 36
Verses On Rebuke. 77
Verses On Redemption. 74
Verses On Regeneration Or A New Birth. 95
Verses On Servants. 59
Verses On Sound Doctrine. 25, 44
Verses On Speaking Evil. 86
Verses On Tychicus. 109
Verses On Unfruitful. 111
Verses On Ungodliness. 66
Verses On Unprofitable. 105
Verses On Unruly. 26
Verses On "Hold Fast". 24
Verses On "Set In Order". 11
Verses On "The Faith" And Doctrine. 33
Verses That Menton Titus. 8
Website: www.BibleForToday.org. I
WILLING TO BE GODLY BRINGS PERSECUTION. 69
Without children, a man should not be a pastor or a deacon. 14
without fruit. 111
Words of God. .... iii, 4, 7, 15, 22, 23, 36, 42, 43, 58, 59, 69,
                                          84, 87, 88, 96, 101, 106
Young Christian Men Should Be Sober Minded. 53
Young Women To Be Discreet. 51
YOUTHFUL LUSTS ARE NOT LIMITED TO YOUTH. 68

About The Author

The author of this book, Dr. D. A. Waite, received a B.A. (Bachelor of Arts) in classical Greek and Latin from the University of Michigan in 1948, a Th.M. (Master of Theology), with high honors, in New Testament Greek Literature and Exegesis from Dallas Theological Seminary in 1952, an M.A. (Master of Arts) in Speech from Southern Methodist University in 1953, a Th.D. (Doctor of Theology), with honors, in Bible Exposition from Dallas Theological Seminary in 1955, and a Ph.D. in Speech from Purdue University in 1961. He held both New Jersey and Pennsylvania teacher certificates in Greek and Language Arts.

He has been a teacher in the areas of Greek, Hebrew, Bible, Speech, and English for over thirty-five years in ten schools, including one junior high, one senior high, four Bible institutes, two colleges, two universities, and one seminary. He served his country as a Navy Chaplain for five years on active duty; was the pastor of three churches; was Chairman and Director of the Radio and Audio-Film Commission of the American Council of Christian Churches; since 1969, has been Founder, President, and Director of THE BIBLE FOR TODAY; since 1978, has been Founder and President of the DEAN BURGON SOCIETY; has produced over 700 other studies, books, audio cassettes, CD's, or VCR's on various topics; and is heard IN DEFENSE OF TRADITIONAL BIBLE TEXTS and verse-by-verse preaching, by streaming on the Internet at BibleForToday.org, 24/7/365 on the BROWN BOX.

Dr. and Mrs. Waite have been married since 1948; they have four sons, one daughter, and, at present, eight grandchildren, and fifteen great-grandchildren. Since October 4, 1998, he has been the Pastor of the BIBLE FOR TODAY BAPTIST CHURCH in Collingswood, New Jersey. His sermons are heard on the Internet over www.BibleForToday.org on the BROWN BOX.

Order Blank (p. 1)

Name:_____
Address:_____
City & State:_____ Zip:_____
Credit Card #:_____ Expires:_____

Verse by Verse Preaching Books By Dr. D. A. Waite

[ ] Send Titus–Preaching Verse By Verse By Pastor D. A. Waite, (142 pages ($15.00 + $7.00 S&H) fully indexed.
[ ] Send James–Preaching Verse By Verse By Pastor D. A. Waite, (218 pages (16.00 + $7.00 S&H) fully indexed.
[ ] Send *1,2, & 3 John–Preaching Verse By Verse* By Pastor D. A. Waite, 202 pages ($14.00 + $7.00 S&H) fully indexed.
[ ] Send *2 Peter & Jude–Preaching Verse By Verse* By Pastor D. A. Waite, 237 pages ($16.00 +$7.00 S&H) fully indexed.
[ ] Send *1 & 2 Thessalonians–Preaching Verse By Verse* By Pastor D. A. Waite, 360 pages ($20.00 + $8.00 S&H) fully indexed.
[ ] Send *Hebrews–Preaching Verse by Verse*, By Pastor D. A. Waite, 616 pages ($34.00 +$10.00 S&H) fully indexed.
[ ] Send *Revelation–Preaching Verse by Verse*, By Pastor D. A. Waite, 1032 pages ($55.00 + $10.00 S&H) fully indexed.
[ ] Send *1 Timothy--Preaching Verse by Verse*, by Pastor D. A. Waite, 288 pages, hardback ($18+$7 S&H) fully indexed.
[ ] Send *2 Timothy--Preaching Verse by Verse*, by Pastor D. A. Waite, 250 pages, hardback ($16+$7 S&H) fully indexed.
[ ] Send *Romans--Preaching Verse by Verse* by Pastor D. A. Waite 736 pp. Hardback ($35+$8 S&H) fully indexed
[ ] Send *Colossians & Philemon--Preaching Verse by Verse* by Pastor D. A. Waite ($16+$7 S&H) hardback, 240 pages.
[ ] Send *Philippians--Preaching Verse by Verse* by Pastor D A. Waite ($14+$7 S&H) hardback, 176 pages. fully indexed.

Send or Call Orders to:
THE BIBLE FOR TODAY
900 Park Ave., Collingswood, NJ 08108
Phone: 856-854-4452; FAX:--2464; Orders: 1-800 JOHN 10:9
E-Mail Orders: BFT@BibleForToday.org; Credit Cards OK

Order Blank (p. 2)

Name:_____
Address:_____
City & State:_____ Zip:_____
Credit Card #:_____ Expires:_____

[ ] Send *Ephesians--Preaching Verse by Verse* by Pastor D. A. Waite ($15+$7 S&H) hardback, 224 pages. fully indexed.

[ ] Send *Galatians--Preaching Verse By Verse* by Pastor D. A. Waite ($15+$7 S&H) hardback, 216 pages. fully indexed.

[ ] Send *1 Peter–Preaching Verse By Verse* by Pastor D. A. Waite ($15.00 + $7.00 S&H) pages. fully indexed.

Other Books By Dr. D. A. Waite

[ ] Send *A Critical Answer to God's Word Preserved* by Pastor D. A. Waite, 192 pp. perfect bound ($11.00+$4.00 S&H)

[ ] Send *Defending the King James Bible* by DAW ($12+$5 S&H) A hardback book, indexed with study questions.

[ ] Send *BJU's Errors on Bible Preservation* by Dr. D. A. Waite, 110 pages, paperback ($8+$4 S&H) fully indexed

[ ] Send *Fundamentalist Deception on Bible Preservation* by Dr. D. A. Waite, ($8+$4 S&H), paperback, fully indexed

[ ] Send *Fundamentalist MIS-INFORMATION on Bible Versions* by Dr. Waite ($7+$4 S&H) perfect bound, 136 pages

[ ] Send *Fundamentalist Distortions on Bible Versions* by Dr. Waite ($6+$3 S&H) A perfect bound book, 80 pages

[ ] Send *Fuzzy Facts From Fundamentalists* by Dr. D. A. Waite ($8.00 + $4.00) printed booklet

[ ] Send *Foes of the King James Bible Refuted* by DAW ($10 +$4 S&H) A perfect bound book, 164 pages in length.

[ ] Send *Central Seminary Refuted on Bible Versions* by Dr. Waite ($10+$4 S&H) A perfect bound book, 184 pages

[ ] Send *Westcott's Denial of Resurrection*, Dr. Waite ($4+$3)

[ ] Send *Four Reasons for Defending KJB* by DAW ($3+$3)

Send or Call Orders to:
THE BIBLE FOR TODAY
900 Park Ave., Collingswood, NJ 08108
Phone: 856-854-4452; FAX:--2464; Orders: 1-800 JOHN 10:9
E-Mail Orders: BFT@BibleForToday.org; Credit Cards OK

Order Blank (p. 3)

Name:_____
Address:_____
City & State:_____Zip:_____
Credit Card #:_____Expires:_____

[ ] Send *Holes in the Holman Christian Standard Bible* by Dr. Waite ($3+$2 S&H) A printed booklet, 40 pages
[ ] Send *Contemporary Eng. Version Exposed*, DAW ($3+$2)
[ ] Send *NIV Inclusive Language Exposed* by DAW ($5+$3)
[ ] Send *26 Hours of KJB Seminar* (4 videos) by DAW($50.00)
[ ] Send *Making Marriage Melodious* by Pastor D. A. Waite ($7+$4 S&H), perfect bound, 112 pages.
[ ] Send *Burgon's Warnings on Revision* by DAW ($7+$4 S&H) A perfect bound book, 120 pages in length.
[ ] Send *The Superior Foundation of the KJB* By Dr. D. A. Waite ($10.00 + $7.00 S&H)
[ ] Send *Biblical Separation–1,896 Bible Verses About It* by Dr. D. A. Waite ($14.00 + $7.00 S&H)
[ ] Send *Westcott & Hort's Greek Text & Theory Refuted by Burgon's Revision Revised--Summarized* by Dr. D. A. Waite ($7.00+$4 S&H), 120 pages, perfect bound.
[ ] Send *Dean Burgon's Confidence in KJB* by DAW ($3+$3)
[ ] Send *Vindicating Mark 16:9-20* by Dr. Waite ($3+$3S&H)
[ ] Send *Summary of Traditional Text* by Dr. Waite ($3 +$3)
[ ] Send *Summary of Causes of Corruption*, DAW ($3+$3)
[ ] Send *Summary of Inspiration* by Dr. Waite ($3+$3 S&H)
[ ] Send *Soulwinning's Versions-Perversions* By Dr. D. A. Waite ($6.00 + $5.00 S&H)
[ ] Send *The Case for the King James Bible* by DAW ($7 +$3 S&H) A perfect bound book, 112 pages in length.
[ ] Send *Theological Heresies of Westcott and Hort* by Dr. D. A. Waite, ($7+$3 S&H) A printed booklet.

Send or Call Orders to:
THE BIBLE FOR TODAY
900 Park Ave., Collingswood, NJ 08108
Phone: 856-854-4452; FAX:--2464; Orders: 1-800 JOHN 10:9
E-Mail Orders: BFT@BibleForToday.org; Credit Cards OK

Order Blank (p. 4)

Name:_____
Address:_____
City & State:_____Zip:_____
Credit Card #:_____Expires:_____

Books By Dr. Jack Moorman

[ ] Send *Samuel P. Tregelles--The Man Who Made the Critical Text Acceptable to Bible Believers* by Dr. Moorman ($2+$1)

[ ] Send *8,000 Differences Between TR & CT* by Dr. Jack Moorman [$65 + $7.50 S&H] Over 500-large-pages of data

[ ] Send *356 Doctrinal Errors in the NIV & Other Modern Versions*, 100-large-pages, $10.00+$6 S&H.

[ ] Send *The Doctrinal Heart of the Bible--Removed from Modern Versions* by Dr. Jack Moorman, VCR, $15 +$4 S&H

[ ] Send *Modern Bibles--The Dark Secret* by Dr. Jack Moorman, $5+$3 S&H

Books By Dean John William Burgon

[ ] Send *The Revision Revised* by Dean Burgon ($25 + $5 S&H) A hardback book, 640 pages in length.

[ ] Send *The Last 12 verses of Mark* by Dean Burgon ($15+$5 S&H) A hardback book 400 pages.

[ ] Send *The Traditional Text* hardback by Burgon ($16+$5 S&H) A hardback book, 384 pages in length.

[ ] Send *Causes of Corruption* by Burgon ($15+$5 S&H) A hardback book, 360 pages in length.

[ ] Send *Inspiration and Interpretation*, Dean Burgon ($25+$5 S&H) A hardback book, 610 pages in length.

Send or Call Orders to:
THE BIBLE FOR TODAY
900 Park Ave., Collingswood, NJ 08108
Phone: 856-854-4452; FAX:--2464; Orders: 1-800 JOHN 10:9
E-Mail Orders: BFT@BibleForToday.org; Credit Cards OK

Order Blank (p. 5)

Name:_____
Address:_____
City & State:_____Zip:_____
Credit Card #:_____Expires:_____

Books By Miscellaneous Authors

[ ] Send *Scrivener's <u>Annotated</u> Greek New Testament*, by Dr. Frederick Scrivener: Hardback--($35+$5 S&H); Genuine Leather--($45+$5 S&H)

[ ] Send *Why Not the King James Bible?--An Answer to James White's KJVO Book* by Dr. K. D. DiVietro, $10+$5 S&H

[ ] Send Brochure #1: "*1000 Titles Defending the KJB/TR*" No Charge

[ ] Send *The LIE That Changed the Modern World* by Dr. H. D. Williams ($16+$5 S&H) Hardback book

[ ] Send *With Tears in My Heart* by Gertrude G. Sanborn. Hardback 414 pp. ($25+$5 S&H) 400 Christian Poems

[ ] Send *Able To Bear It* By Gertrude Sanborn ($14.00 + $7.00 S&H

[ ] Send *When the KJB Departs from the So-Called "Majority Text"* by Dr. Jack Moorman, $16+$5 S&H

[ ] Send *Missing in Modern Bibles--Nestle-Aland/NIV Errors* by Dr. Jack Moorman, $8+$4 S&H

[ ] Send *Guide to Textual Criticism* by Edward Miller ($7+$4) Hardback book

[ ] Send *Scrivener's Greek New Testament Underlying the King James Bible*, hardback, ($14+$5 S&H)

[ ] Send *The Manuscript Digest of the N.T.* (721 pp.) By Dr. Jack Moorman, copy-machine bound ($50+$7 S&H)

[ ] *Early Manuscripts, Church Fathers, & the Authorized Version* by Dr. Jack Moorman, $18+$5 S&H. Hardback

[ ] Send *Forever Settled--Bible Documents & History Survey* by Dr. Jack Moorman, $20+$5 S&H. Hardback book.

Send or Call Orders to:
THE BIBLE FOR TODAY
900 Park Ave., Collingswood, NJ 08108
Phone: 856-854-4452; FAX:--2464; Orders: 1-800 JOHN 10:9
E-Mail Orders: BFT@BibleForToday.org; Credit Cards OK

Order Blank (p. 6)

Name:_____
Address:_____
City & State:_____Zip:_____
Credit Card #:_____Expires:_____

[ ] Send *English Standard Bible (ESV) Deficiencies* By several authors ($7.00 + $4.00 S&H)
[ ] Send *Strong's Micro-Print Concordance* By the Sherbornes ($21.00 + $8.00 S&H)
[ ] Send *The Doctored New Testament* by D. A. Waite, Jr. ($25+$5 S&H) Greek MSS differences shown, hardback
[ ] Send *Readability of A.V. (KJB)* by D. A. Waite, Jr. ($6+$3)
[ ] Send *4,114 Definitions from the Defined King James Bible* by D. A. Waite, Jr. ($7.00+$4.00 S&H)
[ ] Send *Visitation In Action* By Mr. R. O. Sanborn ($10.00 + $7.00 S&H)
[ ] Send *Daily Bible Blessings From Daily Bible Readings* By Yvonne Sanborn Waite ($30.00 + $10.00 S&H)
[ ] Send *Husband-Loving Lessons* By Yvonne Sanborn Waite ($25.00 + $8.00 S&H)
[ ] Send *Gnosticism–The Doctrinal Foundation of New Bibles* by J. Moser ($20.00 + $8.00 S&H)
[ ] Send *Dean Burgon's Defense of the Authorised Version* By Dr. David Bennett ($14.0 + 8.00 S&H)
[ ] Send *Drift in Baptist Missions, Churches & Schools* by Dr. David Bennett ($12.00 + $8.00 S&H)
[ ] Send *God's Marvelous Book* By Dr. David Bennett ($15.00 + $8.00 S&H)
[ ] Send *CCM Not The Problem–Only A Symptom* By Dr. David Bennett ($12.00 + $7.00 S&H)

Send or Call Orders to:
THE BIBLE FOR TODAY
900 Park Ave., Collingswood, NJ 08108
Phone: 856-854-4452; FAX:--2464; Orders: 1-800 JOHN 10:9
E-Mail Orders: BFT@BibleForToday.org; Credit Cards OK

Order Blank (p. 7)

Name:_____
Address:_____
City & State:_____ Zip:_____
Credit Card #:_____ Expires:_____

Question And Answer Books By Dr. D. A. Waite

[ ] Send *The First 200 Questions Answered* By Dr. D. A. Waite ($15.00 + $7.00 S&H)

[ ] Send *The Second 200 Questions Answered* By Dr. D. A. Waite ($15.00 + $7.00 S&H)

[ ] Send *The Third 200 Questions Answered* By Dr. D. A. Waite ($15.00 + $7.00 S&H)

[ ] Send *The Fourth 200 Questions Answered* By Dr. D. A. Waite ($15.00 + $7.00 S&H)

[ ] Send *The Fifth 200 Questions Answered* By Dr. D. A. Waite ($15.00 + $7.00 S&H)

[ ] Send *The Sixth 200 Questions Answered* By Dr. D. A. Waite ($15.00 + $7.00 S&H)

Send or Call Orders to:
THE BIBLE FOR TODAY
900 Park Ave., Collingswood, NJ 08108
Phone: 856-854-4452; FAX:--2464; Orders: 1-800 JOHN 10:9
E-Mail Orders: BFT@BibleForToday.org; Credit Cards OK

The Defined
King James Bible
Uncommon Words Defined Accurately

I. Deluxe Genuine Leather
✦Large Print--Black or Burgundy✦
1 for $44.00+$12.00 S&H
✦Case of 12 for✦
$34.00 each+$50.00 S&H
✦Medium Print--Black or Burgundy✦
1 for $39.00+$8.00 S&H
✦Case of 12 for✦
$29.00 each+$40.00 S&H

II. Deluxe Hardback Editions
$17.00 each+$40.00 S&H (Large Print)
1 for $22.00+12.00 S&H (Large Print)
✦Case of 12 for✦
1 for $19.50+$8.00 S&H (Medium Print)
✦Case of 12 for✦
$12.50 each+$30.00 S&H (Medium Print)

Order Phone: 1-800-JOHN 10:9

Credit Cards Welcomed

Pastor D. A. Waite, Th.D., Ph.D.

Paul's Instructions To Pastor Titus

The Importance Of Apostle Paul Instructing Pastor Titus. Pastor Titus was on the lonely island of Crete. There were probably no other New Testament churches on that island at the time. Paul thought it was vital to tell this pastor many important things that he and other pastors should know and tell others about. Pastors today should also know these things.

Paul Told Pastor Titus 15 Standards That Biblical Pastors Must Meet. These 15 standards were not only necessary for pastors in Titus's days to meet, but they must also be fulfilled in our days by those who wish to be pastors. Sad to say, there are hundreds and thousands of today's pastors who do not meet all 15 of these standards. This is a serious compromise and disobedience to God's Words!

Paul Told Pastor Titus To Tell Biblical Pastors To Hold Fast To 4 Things. It is not enough for Pastors to meet all 15 of these Biblical standards. They must also *"hold fast"* to four important things as they minister the Words of God to their congregations. It is just as important for Biblical pastors today to hold fast to these four things so as not to lead their congregations into false doctrines and practices. Pastors must be good examples for those to whom they minister.

Paul Told Four Groups Of People To Do Certain Things. There were 6 things for aged men; 12 things for aged women; 6 things for Pastor Titus; and 5 things that are taught by God's grace. Many of these 29 specific things are completely absent in the lives of people today. Many in these groups--even some genuine Christians--don't read God's Words to know what God expects of them. That leaves them ignorant of God's will.

www.BibleForToday.org

BFT 4166   ISBN #978-1-56848-114-2